Getting Down to Earth

A Call to Environmental Action

John Heidtke

PAULIST PRESS

New York/Mahwah, NJ

 This book is printed on recycled paper.

Interior art by Eileen Martin, O.P.

Photographs are used courtesy of the International Joint Commission.

Copyright © 1993 by John Heidtke

Library of Congress Cataloguing-in-Publication Data

Heidtke, John, 1946-
    Getting down to earth : a call to environmental action / John Heidtke
      p.   cm.
    Includes bibliographical references.
    ISBN 0-8091-9571-2 (paper)
    1. Human ecology–Moral and ethical aspects. 2. Human ecology–Religious aspects–Christianity. 3. Values. 4. Environmental policy–United States–Citizen participation. I. Title.
GF80.H45   1993
363.7'0525–dc20   92-36138
                                                         CIP

Published by Paulist Press
997 Macarthur Boulevard
Mahwah, NJ 07430

Printed and bound in the United States of America

CONTENTS

PART THREE

ECO-VALUES IN ACTION

PART FOUR

RESOURCES

Acknowledgments

There are many individuals who have contributed to my appreciation and understanding of creation and ecological values. I am especially grateful to the following people who shared their ideas, dreams about a greener world, and encouragement.

– Fred Ludwig, M.D., a pioneer Audubon researcher who introduced me to innovative solutions to the environmental problems of the Great Lakes.

– Laura Armour, a representative for the Greyhound Protection League, who freely offered literature on creatures great and small.

– Tim Eder, National Wildlife Federation, who willingly provided information about international water quality projects.

– Ellen Ross, a friend and nature enthusiast, who always urged me to examine environmental issues with a critical eye and openmindedness.

– This book became possible with the assistance and support of certain individuals.

– Kevin A. Lynch, C.S.P., Publisher, Paulist Press, who believed in the need for this book.

– Maria L. Maggi, my editor, who provided guidance and feedback with a wonderful sense of humor.

– Eileen Martin, O.P., an artist and educator, who devoted her gifts and love of nature to furnish many of the illustrations.

– Arlene Rutkowski, a biology teacher, who offered ideas and exercises.

– Toni George, a friend, who typed (and retyped!) the original manuscript.

A special thank you to my wife, Rene, and daughters, Katie and Jeanne, who share a deep appreciation for the out-of-doors.

DEDICATION

This book is dedicated with love to my parents,
Harry and Rufina Heidtke.
They shaped my values and inspired a curiosity about nature.

Preface

No great genius must be consulted to know that our planet and its elegant life-support systems are under terrible stress, nor that humans are the root cause of these problems. The evidence surrounds us. Thoughtful people ask why must it be this way. Did we not learn to care for our friends, siblings, homes, churches, parents? If so, how can we tolerate the destruction of the very earth and its creatures which give us food, water, natural beauty and inspiration? These are *or most certainly should be* very disturbing questions for our young people and their elders. How we fail to recognize the fragility of this earth is a puzzle that we must solve in order to have a future filled with opportunity and personal fulfillment.

Caring for any person, pet, institution, or holding any belief depends on what we choose to value in our daily lives. We are accustomed to valuing possessions in terms of money—the almighty dollar has been our standard all too often. We tend to use the same money values when looking at the natural world. The developer sees the wetland as a way to make more money, if only he can get permits to fill and destroy it. But the wildlife, erosion protection, and the open space of the wetland which nourishes our spirits is seen as valueless. The timber company sees the trees in the forest as many board feet of finished cut lumber worth a dollar a foot. But the spotted owls and other endangered species in the forest have no dollar value. Thus, the old trees the owls need, which also provide some of the best finished lumber, are cut for profit and to provide jobs for a year or two. Again and again we have repeated this basic error of valuing only what is used in human commerce, acting as though the natural world can absorb this plundering of its natural resources for a short-range economic gain.

By themselves, development and short-range use of resources are not necessarily wrong. Much that is good—schools, churches, cities and our culture—has been built by our harvest and use of natural resources. Society as we know it could not exist without use of these natural resources. Thus, our task is to use resources without destroying the ecological systems that provide and renew them for us.

As *human animals*, we are subject to the same biological rules as any other animal. We live lives of a particular length, generally our three score and ten, eat the same sorts of foods as other animals, breathe the same air, detoxify the same pollutants, excrete the same waste products, and reproduce. All these *functions* are basically the same for all animals. What makes us unique and different is that, unlike animals who do not consciously consider the consequences of their actions, we have been given the tools and mandate from God to do this. We are able to ask what it means to cut down a tree, something that the master timbercutter of all animals, the beaver, never asks. For the beaver, cutting down a tree and limbing it for food means a meal and a place to live when the remains of the tree are placed in the beaver's house or dam. That the beaver cut down the spotted owl's nest tree or the home of the flying squirrel was not considered by the beaver. But, God required us to be good stewards when we were given dominion over the earth, its animals and its bounty. Stated another way, we have the *duty* to understand and consider the consequences of our actions on the life in our world. *We must protect the world we live in.* It is that simple.

This duty need not be oppressive nor terribly difficult so long as we learn how to set our values to consider all the costs to nature of our decisions and the hidden benefits that lie obscured behind the usual way of looking at the world.

Sunsets and butterflies tell us that economic gain is but one of the uses we make of the resources of the world. By using our free will to choose, we can have our timber harvests, our spotted owls, our beavers and our flying squirrels through careful choices and balance. But, first we must understand how we set our values, how we place them in action, and what will happen to us and our peers when we forget to live our lives as though we were making important decisions all the time. In fact, the most mundane everyday sorts of decisions we make add up to influence what happens in the natural world. That is what this book is about—everyday lives that are lived by choosing to do what will preserve the life-support systems of our beloved spaceship earth. This means understanding that the values you believe in are to be lived in your daily life. *Getting Down to Earth* explores doing that with care, humility, and the true pride that comes from caring enough to live with reverence in support of all life on earth. Exercise your free will and read on to learn how to set your values in celebration of all life!

James P. Ludwig, Ph.D.
Environmental Educator, Researcher and Consultant

Introduction

- Each summer, more than 1,300 young adults throughout the United States volunteer their time and energy to assist with significant work projects in our national parks and forests.
- Students at Carnegie-Mellon University, Pittsburgh, were shocked to learn about the amount of edible food that was thrown out at their school every day. Their initial concern has grown into a well-organized program to donate food to the hungry.
- In 1988 students marched on City Hall in New York City to demand funding for education on humane animal treatment in every classroom within the New York City public school system.
- Each spring, students at Central Michigan University help sponsor a community-wide "adopt-a-tree" project.

What motivates young adults to become involved in environmental action? There are many reasons. Now that we have heightened our awareness about the environmental crisis, more attention is being given to help remedy the problems. But another dramatic thing is occurring in our society. *Young adults are feeling a deep compassion for the earth.* They feel strongly about saving dolphins from drowning in drift fish nets. They have expressed sensitivity to preserve the earth in massive petition drives to halt oil drilling in Alaska's national forests and to stop a major toy company from testing its toy products on animals. The earth is like a sick patient—stricken by abuse and pollution—and young adults are deeply empathetic to the pain.

Where does this compassion and sensitivity come from? From our ecological values—*eco-values* for short. *Our eco-values guide our thoughts, beliefs, and action about how we treat and respect the earth.* And as we learn to get in touch with these values, we become more sensitive to nature, the meaning of creation, environmental problems, and life on earth. Many of these ecological values are grounded in our Christian faith and beliefs.

As human beings we have always grown faster in technological skills than in values which help guide our decisions about where technology will lead us. We have invented gadgets and machines which pollute the earth and, later, we begin to weigh the values and importance of such ingenuity. The same is true with solving our environmental ills. We have "how to . . ." skills—how to recycle, how to save energy, how to save endangered wildlife. Yet, in many respects, the ecological values which motivate us to use these skills remain a mystery. They are there. We have difficulty identifying our values and talking about them. Part of heightening our awareness about our ecological values is the ability to name and describe them.

Let's look at the situation this way. We put words to a tune and this becomes a song. When music contains words that move us, we enjoy listening to the song over and over. We all have favorite songs that we sing in our heads, so to speak. The same is true with eco-values. When we have a common language that describes our values, we can recognize them and act.

Getting Down to Earth has been written so that your earth-sensitive values become like a song in your head. And you can share this song with others! *Getting Down to Earth* provides readers with an opportunity to know, appreciate, and listen to their ecological values. As readers grow in their awareness of their values they will be able to use their extraordinary energy, talents, and vision to help change how we treat the earth.

Getting Down to Earth is divided into four parts. In Part One readers will gain insights into our environmental crisis. We explore the human attitudes, values, and technological developments that have contributed to our ecological mess. Part Two describes our personal value systems which include our ecological values. This section provides a clear, step-by-step approach to understanding and listening to your ecological values. Strategies help you to define action steps to carry out environmental action. In Part Three you will meet St. Francis of Assisi, John Muir, Henry David Thoreau, Albert Schweitzer, Aldo Leopold, and Rachel Carson. All of these remarkable individuals lived their ecological values to the fullest. Their lives offer us inspiration. Part Four describes environmental resources that you can use. Christians are called to action. "In everything a prudent man acts with knowledge" (Prov 13:16). Environmental resources expand our skills, knowledge, and ability to act.

At the end of this book are ten specific Eco-Ideas. They describe simple yet important ecological activities. As you better understand your eco-values, you might choose to carry out these activities at home, with friends, or at school. Or they might give you ideas for other environmental action.

I hope this book offers you a fresh understanding of ecological values which will contribute to our environmental movement and Christian responsibilities to improve the quality of life in our global community. If we can accomplish this together, then we can become more and more hopeful about the earth's future!

Symbol of Hope

Hearts are symbols of love. The crucifix is a symbol of Christ's redeeming love. A picture of the earth is a symbol of environmentalism. Symbols are visible signs that stand for or suggest something of significance. To me, the common loon is a symbol of hope for the environment.

During the summer of 1988, our family was vacationing in northern Michigan. We had planned to hike in the lush, green forests, but the effects of a drought had turned everything brown and dry. One early morning we hiked into a wildlife refuge. Dawn was breaking and we stopped to watch the mist rise over an inland lake. A moose stood on the distant shoreline. The haunting song of a loon broke the silence. Another hiker standing nearby observed, "If this drought continues, the loon might become extinct. The loon's breeding grounds are being destroyed."

Extinct! The thought was shocking!

Loons are ancient birds. They have existed for over sixty-five million years. Loons have survived all kinds of con-

ditions, including our toxic industrial chemicals which have poisoned lakes and streams. So could the drought be the final assault? As I wondered about that, I felt grief.

There is an Indian legend about an old blind man whose family was starving. In the tale a loon with magical powers appeared and restored the man's sight, and as a result he was able to hunt once again. I thought about this story and how tragic it would be to lose this majestic bird forever. This was a turning point in my environmental awareness. I vowed that these beautiful creatures in God's creation would not lose their right to live.

Throughout this book you will see pictures of loons. They serve as a symbol. I use them as a reminder that the hope for our survival on earth depends on how we respectfully treat nature. It is a sign of how we value nature. And I pass this message with its symbol of hope onto you.

Part One
Our Ecological Crisis:
A Crisis in Human Values

"Most of the luxuries,
and many of the so-called comforts,
of life are not only dispensable,
but hindrances to the elevation of mankind."
—Henry David Thoreau

Our Heightened Awareness

Recently a friend who teaches biology phoned me. We'll call my friend Paul. Paul was upset about an episode that had occurred earlier in one of his classes.

Let me take a moment to summarize our telephone conversation. It contained several points about ecological values that we will explore together.

Paul had given his class a written assignment to answer a question, "What is one thing you can do to help save the earth?" Most of the students returned at least a page of helpful ideas, but two students handed in blank sheets of paper. Paul was taken aback. At first he wanted to know if this was a practical joke. No, the students replied, they were serious. They believed the earth was so polluted that it was beyond saving. One student said, "Even if I tried to do something worthwhile it isn't going to matter."

Paul was dismayed by the students' defeatist attitudes and at a loss to explain their actions. This is why he had called me. He wanted to bounce some questions off me to get my reaction.

This is supposed to be the age of environmental action, Paul said. So why did the two students feel that they lacked power to help remedy the earth's ills? Had he failed to inspire their enthusiasm for environmental action?

I was interested in knowing how the class learned about ecology. Paul described how the students had conducted experiments to observe the earth's functions. They also used creative experiments to see how pollution impacts and destroys the earth's functions.

Apparently the class was very involved in heightening their awareness about the earth and our environmental crisis. I asked if the students had had an opportunity to discuss their ecological values. Paul sounded puzzled and asked what I meant by "ecological values."

I explained that all of us have a collection of personal values. Personal values include standards of right and wrong and beliefs about achievement, freedom, and how we treat each other. *Our value system also includes our beliefs about the earth. These are called ecological values, or eco-values.* Our ecological values consist of *nature-oriented values* and *spiritual eco-values.*

Paul was curious and wanted to know more about ecological values. I explained that nature-oriented values help us to appreciate the beauty and wonder of the natural world. We experience nature-oriented values when we stop to admire a magnificent sunset. Spiritual ecological values bring us closer to God and our responsibility to care for God's creation. We experience spiritual eco-values when we reflect on the meaning of life and creation and we do things to protect the earth.

After listening, Paul said, "I'm beginning to see that my students missed an important step in being concerned about the earth. Maybe we should have talked about our ecological values. It sounds as if values push us to action."

I agreed. Values do guide us to act. If a person values honesty, the truth is spoken. When thrift is valued, people buy reusable goods and help recycle. Values help us to make daily choices and decisions.

Our eco-values guide our thoughts and decisions about how we care about the earth. Eco-values open opportunities for us to be close to God and the mystery of creation. Our senses are opened to the world around us. We become more sensitive to listening to songbirds. Our eyes catch the beauty of the smallest flowers. Our spirits are refreshed by a walk in the woods or along a beach. These are the wonderful benefits of heightening our awareness of our ecological values and the earth.

Environmental
Awareness

For the next thirty days, scan newspapers and maga-zines for *any* articles about the environment. Such an article might discuss environmental problems or actions taken to remedy them, it might mention a new record album or movie that has environmental value as a major theme. Clip out the articles and save them. Try to get as many as possible. You'll be surprised at the large number you will have collected at the end of one month.

Our Ecological Crisis

Have you ever wondered just how great is our ecological mess? When we read about the greenhouse effect, hazardous waste dumps, and vanishing wildlife, what do those expressions really mean? Let's take a look at several "earth facts."

- Humankind's chemical products are destroying the atmosphere's ozone. The ozone is a protective shield that acts like armor against dangerous solar ultraviolet radiation. As the ozone diminishes, the earth is bombarded with ultraviolet radiation. The result? More than one hundred and fifty million more people will get skin cancer in the U.S. alone over the next eighty years.

- Approximately ninety-seven percent of the earth's water supply is sea water. Less than two percent (a mere drop in the bucket!) is surface water available for human use. To date, over seven hundred chemicals have been identified in United States drinking water, and many are dangerous.

- Destruction of forests has triggered worldwide flooding and loss of valuable topsoil. This havoc contributes to global warming. The relentless cutting of forests is destroying land resources crucial to the welfare of humankind. Every Sunday in the U.S. more than five hundred thousand trees are used to produce the eighty-eight percent of newspapers and comics that are not recycled.

- Over eighty thousand chemicals are in common use today, and about one thousand new chemicals enter into commercial use each year. While humanity has benefited enormously from the use of chemicals, there is a dark side to the story. Toxic substances in pesticides and fertilizers pollute the earth. Many common household products like oven cleaners contain dangerous substances. Used products are discarded in landfills and the substances seep into the groundwater. Every year over two hundred thousand American children who drink heavily leaded water experience a significant loss of brain function.

The impact of pollution on human health is not a recent phenomenon. In the late 1950s, some scientists had documented how environmental ills affect birds, fish, and trees. They predicted that some day human health would be seriously impaired as well. Today this is occurring and the results, as we have just seen, are disastrous.

How could this happen? Why didn't we use our fundamental knowledge about the environment to prevent this ecological crisis?

To answer these questions we need to explore three issues that have influenced how we, as an industrial society, have interacted with the environment and the values that have guided us. We need to examine:

1. our country's history of environmental action;

2. our view of the earth and how we have treated the environment;

3. the lack of ecological value education in our schools and other institutions.

As we explore these issues, we will see that one of the threads that weaves through all of this is human values. Christians have always been confronted with the question about the sacredness of life. What is the Christian's responsibility to protect life? Now we must take these questions a step further. The ecological disasters which have evolved are forcing us to rethink how we treat the planet's air, water, plant, and wildlife systems. Our environmental crisis is a result of misguided human values.

Historical View

In the United States the greatest gain in the environmental movement occurred after 1960. When you think about it, that wasn't all that long ago! During the late 1960s, television was bringing the dramatic tragedies of environmental pollution into public awareness. People were sickened by the ugly sight of oil spills that were ruining beaches and killing marine wildlife. Also, there was growing public concern over air pollution, commonly called smog. TV cameras recorded thick blankets of smog choking cities. Suddenly the United States woke up to an environmental nightmare.

Seeds of Faulty Thinking

Of course, things were not always this way in America. Or so we thought! During our early history, most Americans lived in uncrowded rural areas. People did not have pollution-causing machines, gadgets, or motor vehicles. While most people did not face a serious pollution problem, they carried the seeds of faulty misconceptions about the earth that eventually contributed to future environmental headaches. Early Americans believed that they could conquer nature. The earth's resources existed to supply human needs and pleasures. These attitudes often led to an exploitation of the earth's resources. European settlers were on the move, and anything in their way, including trees and wildlife, was mowed down. Naturalists like Henry David Thoreau who protested these beliefs were seen as oddballs. Thoreau did not become an environmental hero until after Earth Day 1970 when his writing became very popular.

Earth Day Awareness

Earth Day 1970 became a milestone in our anti-pollution movement. On April 22, 1970 more than twenty million people throughout the United States participated in environmental demonstrations, lectures, and earth fairs. With the outpouring of such public sentiment, one would think that the tide against waste and polluting activity would turn. In some respects this happened. Congress passed significant legislation for clean air and water. People participated in community clean-up campaigns. Membership in environmental organizations increased. Solar energy became popular in the mind of the public. But in other ways, it was business as usual. We did not radically change our beliefs and misconceptions about the earth. We filled up our garbage dumps with throwaway gadgets and materials. Industry pumped invisible toxic chemicals into the air, water, and soil. We turned nature into a resource to be used to satisfy our own, often frivolous, appetites.

Dr. Fraser Darling, known as the world's "pioneer ecologist," observed how the nation's media saturated the public's mind with the word *ecology* on Earth Day. Knowing how fickle Americans can be, he feared that the public would become sick of the word before they knew what it meant. He also worried that environmentalism might be treated like a fad.

Dr. Darling's anxious concerns were not unfounded. Twenty years later history repeated itself. Once again Earth Day was celebrated. Once again Congress hotly debated legislation aimed to further protect the air, water, and endangered species. This was a senate and gubernatorial election year, so the environmental agendas and political stakes were in high gear. Elections could be won or lost by ecology-minded voters. But when Earth Day 1990 faded from the media headlines, thoughtful environmentalists seriously questioned the value of the event.

The basic message of Earth Day '90 stressed individual responsibility and wise consumer choices. We were instructed to shop in earth-friendly ways. Yet for all the hype, the earth event failed to address how corporate America has successfully manipulated consumer demand and values, shaping our addiction to how our economy is addicted to huge military expenditures, life threatening chemicals, and oil. Earth Day should have been a call to activism. Instead it fell short on meaningful action and inspiration. Our misguided values remained in crisis.

So why can't we seem to effectively remedy our environmental ills? The answer goes back to how our forefathers settled this continent. Once again we need to look at values which have been passed along from generation to generation.

Territorial Expansionism

America the beautiful has also meant America the bountiful. From the beginning, the new world was seen as a blessed land of inexhaustible resources. During the nineteenth century the majority of territory claimed by the United States government was wilderness. With the use of railroads and steamboats Americans were on the move. They were expanding their territorial boundaries westward. Holes were drilled into the earth by mining industries. Forests were cleared for farming and new cities. *There was a prevailing myth that there was plenty of room for people and nature.* As a nation forging its way into the world, America seemed boundless and the ideals of progress became synonymous with territorial expansionism. The value of living harmoniously with nature was incompatible with nineteenth century American priorities.

To believe that early America did not have environmental problems is false. We have a romantic notion of how the wild west was tamed. I believe that the values and misguided thinking and attitudes that have led to our present ecology crisis are symbolized in the tragic decline of buffalo herds. The human thoughts, values, and actions which have endangered the bison also endanger all of us.

When we think about the land where the old buffalo roamed, we usually picture the wild west. But at one time bison populated the midwestern states too. Throughout the land bison were slaughtered by early European settlers, bringing them to near extinction by 1900. Today small herds of buffalo exist in Yellowstone National Park and at some of our nation's zoological parks.

The fate of the buffalo is not settled. For a variety of political reasons, cattle ranchers and hunters are allowed to kill any bison that happen to roam outside the boundaries of Yellowstone National Park. Bison often wander about as part of their natural winter migration. Unwittingly the National Park Service is partially responsible for the bisons' winter wandering. Yellowstone has become a favorite recreational playground, especially for snowmobiles. The time-honored assumption that land is for the sole use of human interests still prevails.

Dominion over Nature

As wagon trains pushed west, settlers carried a deep-seated belief that man could dominate nature. The west was seen as a wild land to be tamed.

How did the settlers acquire such a notion that they could conquer nature? When we try to understand people's values and beliefs it is important to study their history and culture. In order to appreciate how early Americans thought about the earth, we have to look at many ancient beliefs that were handed down through the ages.

Ancient civilizations slowly advanced to agricultural societies. People stopped wandering the earth in tribes. They settled down in farming communities. They exercised a new power over the earth as they used sharp tools to till the soil and plant seeds for food. These ancient groups gained a sense of control over their lives. This shaped how they began to think about nature. The earth was seen as a giant garden. Humankind had dominion over the garden. In time, this led to the belief that people had control over nature.

When we see how attitudes and values are handed down through the ages, we can begin to appreciate why it is difficult to change people's misconceptions about the earth. Even today many people believe that humans have dominion over nature. The near extinction of rain forests is a tragic example of this misguided thinking. We do not always conserve and manage the earth's resources wisely.

Civil Rights and Species Rights

The American Revolution opened a floodgate of idealism based on natural-rights philosophy. Yet for the next century the young nation focused its attention exclusively on the oppression of black slaves. Natural rights idealists realized that human freedom had to be granted first before the rights of nature could even be taken seriously. The abolitionists in Congress would have been foolhardy to have passed legislation forbidding cruelty to animals while millions of black human beings were being treated like livestock. Even Thoreau, a staunch abolitionist, spotted the inconsistency of the matter. Thoreau pointed out the inconsistency of a president of an anti-slavery organization sporting a beaver-skin coat!

After the civil rights movement had guided major social and rights legislation in the 1960s, the nation could turn to other wrongs. The environmental activists borrowed language and tactics from the civil rights organizations. Environmental groups like Greenpeace used the principles of civil disobedience to demonstrate against industrial and corporate evils and their abuse of nature and earth resources. Animal rights organizations became more outspoken about wildlife deserving humane treatment. Groups like People for the Ethical Treatment of Animals (PETA) declared that animals have the right to live free from human cruelty and exploitation.

Animal activists have pushed for legislation guaranteeing animals the right to live free from human exploitation and abuse. This includes banning animal testing for commercial products like cosmetics, lotions, and shampoos.

Many companies no longer make products that are tested on animals. (See Resources for more information.)

Bending Environmental Laws

Our nation has passed numerous laws to help protect the environment. There is legislation to reduce pollution, preserve wetlands and fragile sand dunes, and save wildlife. Yet despite these outstanding achievements and laws, there are still old attitudes and beliefs that humanity can dominate nature. And when people believe that they can control nature, they are tempted to use the earth's resources solely for human satisfaction and pleasure. To accomplish this, environmental laws get twisted and modified so that they become weakened. Weak laws lack effective protection. Weak environmental laws allow people to abuse and exploit the earth.

Let me tell you what happened where I live. Recently a national retail chain planned to build a giant discount store in the community. They wanted to locate the store on wetlands. This created quite a furor. Environmentalists protested the loss of fragile wetland. Pro-developers said that our community needed jobs and progress. They solicited a state senator's support. The senator agreed that unemployment was unacceptable and that the wetland law needed a little bending to accommodate economic growth. Later he dropped that statement when he was reminded that ecology-minded voters were monitoring his public remarks! Environmentalists pointed out to the retailer's corporate office that the proposed store had a reputation of marketing earth-friendly products. Was there a possible contradiction in the message that big business was giving to the community? The retailer decided that the wetland controversy wasn't worth the aggravation and took its plans elsewhere. The wetlands are still surviving. The pro-developers continue to figure out ways to chip away at environmental laws that protect ecosystems.

Whether we have weak or strong environmental laws depends on our priorities—what we believe is most important. We will decide this by following our ecological values and standards of right and wrong behavior.

Single-Minded Thinking About the Earth

Picture this for a moment. Let's say that mother nature goes to a physician for a physical examination. You know, mother nature has felt a little stressed and run-down. What do you think would be the outcome? I would surmise that without hesitation or further diagnostic testing, the physician would rush mother nature to an intensive care unit for immediate treatment!

The earth's physical life support systems—air, water soil, plant and animal life—are in critical condition. As a result, human life, which is a part of the earth's ecosystem, is also jeopardized and plagued with serious health problems.

For a medical team to restore mother nature back to health, they would need to understand the proper ingredients vital for ecological health. They would have to have an astute knowledge of how all of the ecosystems (which are similar to the major organs of the human body) function. It would be imperative to also know how these ecosystems are intimately connected so the earth can function in harmony. Just as the human heart, liver, and kidneys work cooperatively, so must the earth's atmosphere, water, wetlands, plants, and species function interdependently and in a coordinated fashion.

Single-Minded Thinking

To see how all of the major body parts function together is to have a gestalt picture of the body. Gestalt means whole or complete. Gestalt is a way of seeing things in broad terms in order to understand the whole.

In our society, we do not like to think in a gestalt way about things. We often think single-mindedly. Sometimes we get so hung up seeing only one, narrow part of a picture that we miss appreciating the whole. We do this with human health as well as with ecological health.

Go to any bookstore and survey the do-it-yourself books on wellness. You will likely find exercise books showing you how to flatten your tummy or fanny in thirty days flat (no pun intended). This is called "spot reduction" for trimming up the body. This exercise program runs counter to fundamental knowledge about human physiology. The human body needs a total exercise regime. Yet many people prefer to think single-mindedly about exercise. So a lot of money gets spent on these books and programs, regardless of the long-term benefits.

We use the same single-minded approach to ecological health. We tend to think about the earth in its parts, rather than a whole, living system. We dissect the earth as if it were a frog in a biology class. We fail to see that the atmosphere, oceans, lakes, and rivers, flowers and trees, birds and wild creatures and even worms are all connected in a big picture called ecology or nature.

When people do not have a fundamental knowledge about the earth's systems, they are left to think about ecology in what might be called a "media focus." Whatever is "hot" or a priority in the media news becomes the public's preoccupation. Hence, if saving whales hits the headlines, then this absorbs people's interest and environmental activity. Helping whales will later be replaced by some other news story: global warming, tuna drift nets, and fur coat protests. The problem with all of this is that people only get bits and pieces of facts about a complex environmental crisis. Their thinking about the earth remains rather shallow. People fail to grasp the real ecological problems and how sick ecosystems impact each other. People become frustrated because our environmental problems do not disappear.

Ecosystems

Let's examine how the earth's ecosystems function. It is important to keep in mind that all systems must work in *balance*. There are four great ecosystems that help support life on earth. The ecosystems are commonly known as rocks and soil, water, atmosphere, plants and animals. *If any one of these ecosystems is significantly impaired, then severe consequences are sure to occur.* Also, if any one of these ecosystems becomes incompatible with the other forces, major ecological problems will follow. For example, toxic pollution in the Great Lakes and severe drought in Florida have crippled the breeding grounds for ducks, loons, and other migrating birds. Our environmental crisis is the collective result of many such events which cause a severe imbalance in the earth's ecosystems.

Here is a summary of the four major ecosystems of the earth. The key is to recognize their interdependence on each other.

Rocks and Soil

The planet's surface is the basic setting for all life forms. Its complex soil chemistries dictate the kinds and numbers of plants that will grow. Mountains influence weather patterns. Every living organism makes some contribution, positively or negatively, to the soil's chemistry.

Insecticides sprayed on the soil and crops threaten the safety of our food, ground water, and health. Overuse and abuse of the land by mining, oil exploration, and logging industries have led to serious degradation of enormous tracts of U.S. public lands and coastal areas. Overgrazing by cattle producers has left western rangelands barren. Soil erosion impairs other ecosystems. Diverse plant life is lost, and there are reduced food supplies and habitat for deer, elk, and a variety of other wildlife. Many Americans and governmental officials continue to believe erroneously in the importance of expansionism and that land is primarily for human interests.

Water

Water is a miraculous compound that plants, animals, and humans need to exist. Water is a medium for transporting waste and chemicals from one end of the earth to another. Since water can assume the quality of a gas, it can readily move about in the atmosphere. For this reason no one is immune to the ecological problems of a neighboring country—no matter what the geographic distance. Toxic chemicals in the Great Lakes waters are carried on the global winds to pollute the fishing waters of Europe and Japan as well as other distant coastal regions.

Atmosphere

The atmosphere is the blanket of diverse and complex gases that surround the earth, including the air needed by living organisms. It is both a storehouse and a vast distribution system for the oxygen produced by green plants. The atmosphere is the roof of the earth, shielding the planet from cosmic radiation. We have already discussed the major problems of ozone depletion.

Plants and Animals

All life is interrelated. No cell or plant or animal species, including the human species, can exist in complete isolation. As John Muir once observed, everything in the universe and on the earth is hitched to something else. This is certainly seen with plants and animals. Biologists call plant and animal species the biosphere.

Plant and animal species must be diverse in order to thrive and reproduce. When a plant or animal species becomes extinct, there is a rippling effect throughout the ecosystems. This is equally true for the rain forests and wolf populations and any other plant or animal species that is hurt by human activity.

Wetlands destruction is one of the most dramatic effects of human activity in the biosphere. Wetlands act like the human kidney, filtering toxics from the soil and helping to purify waterways. But the wetlands are being wiped out by farming and economic development interests as well as by drought. Dwindling wetlands strip away prime breeding grounds for waterfowl. In 1970 there were an estimated ninety-two million ducks migrating in North America. By 1989 their numbers had fallen to some sixty-four million.

We cannot forget about fish when we discuss the biosphere. Of particular interest are the fresh-water fish that feed off insects which breed on the water's surface. There are also fish which feed off vegetation and sediment on the bottoms of lakes and streams. In the aquatic food chain, bottom feeding fish are also prey to ducks, common loons, and other waterfowl. Toxic chemicals and acid rain lace the sediment and floor vegetation of the Great Lakes. Researchers have documented the connection between declining eagle and common loon populations and heavy toxic contamination in the Great Lakes. Similar problems of toxic pollution kill birds and wildlife in Canada and Europe and as far away as Japan. All corners of the earth are impacted.

Our environmental crisis is largely a result of human interference and destruction of the earth's ecosystems. We have used the earth's resources as if this planet is our sole property or possession. We have failed to realize that the earth belongs to God. From a spiritual and gestalt view, we do not own the earth—we are one part of the whole planet. We are connected to all parts of nature. We breathe the same air as all creatures breathe. We drink from the same sources of water. We are all part of the web of life. Like a giant spider web every form of life is connected in some way. So it is important that we search in the human mind and spirit for ecological values that bring us closer to the sacredness of God's creation.

Experience the Environment	At this point I would like you to STOP and experience what we have been discussing. I would invite you to take a long walk in the outdoors. As you walk, open your senses. Experience the air currents, the temperature, and weather conditions. Feel the warmth of the sun. Carefully listen to the diverse sounds of nature. Look about and see nature's colors, vegetation, and water systems. Depending on the season, watch for small creatures, insects, and maybe even butterflies. Observe how all of the ecosystems come together, interact, and rely on each other. No matter if you are taking a stroll around your neighborhood or a walk in a park or down a country road, open yourself to the world around. How are you, with your values, a part of this natural world?

All parts of the earth are connected and make up a whole, living system.

Toxic chemicals are often used to kill insects.

Industries pump harmful chemicals into the atmosphere which eventually affect all ecosystems.

Abandoned toxic dumps leak pollutants into the soil and our groundwater systems.

Our throw-away society has produced more waste than our landfills can handle.

Toxic chemicals which are dumped into our lakes and rivers kill fish and other forms of marine life.

Lack of Eco-Value Education ───────────────

How do we acquire our values about ecology? How does fighting for animal rights, recycling, energy conservation, and being concerned about nature become part of our lifestyle and personal value system?

There are several important factors in our society that contribute to our eco-values, attitudes, and perceptions of nature: family experiences; school and educational opportunities; church and spiritual experiences; mass media; politics; cultural rituals and habits. Combined, all of these factors shape and mold our thoughts, feelings, and values which guide our behaviors, habits, and the common ways in which we interact with the world around us.

Without a doubt, formal education shapes a student's budding value system. Educational institutions reflect what happens to our society. Students not only absorb the Three Rs but also the formal and informal teachings about nature. Further, students learn the importance of ecology by how it is prioritized in the educational system. Frequently an individual's exposure to knowledge about ecology is limited. It is not uncommon for a student's nature studies to be dependent on the importance a teacher places on the subject. In turn, this may depend on the teacher's knowledge of ecology and enthusiasm to stimulate the student's curiosity about the earth.

Limited Environmental Education

By and large, our school system has produced a limited ecology curriculum. This isn't surprising when we realize that formal education mimics deep-seated priorities, attitudes, prejudices, and values in society.

In his landmark book, *A Sand Country Almanac* (1949), Aldo Leopold observed that American education seemed to deliberately avoid ecological education in its curriculum. He proposed that the country needed a comprehensive approach to ecology. Rather than one course labeled "ecology," ecological concepts needed to be addressed in botany, geography, history, and economics. Overall he felt that ecological training was scarce.

In the 1950s America was fighting communism. Winning the cold war was a national priority. Our government, educators, and conservationists abandoned Aldo Leopold's bold vision for comprehensive ecological education. Instead, science and math dominated school curriculums. Students often learned about ecology in a single class presentation on earth science, and they took nature walks to identify birds and wildflowers. But overall, they did not receive a broad understanding of the environment and environmental problems. Nor did they discuss human values and prejudices which contributed to pollution. During the 1960s America was busy exploring new space frontiers. By the 1970s neglect of the environment was emerging. Earth Day 1970 changed how Americans and educational institutions thought about ecology. Many educators began to look at the written works of Aldo Leopold, Rachel Carson, and Albert Schweitzer for guidance. They wanted to broaden students' understanding of the earth and human values which shape life on this planet. Educators realized that it would be futile to land space ships on the moon while life on earth was endangered.

Comprehensive Eco-Value Education
Today we can participate in many activities to heighten our awareness about ecology and human values which affect life on earth. We have come to realize that environmental education is not confined to the classroom. There are diverse opportunities for learning. These include volunteer activities, visiting nature centers, and joining an environmental group.

Volunteer Activities: There are countless ways to volunteer one's talents at school, at church, and in the community. Helping hands are needed in clean-up campaigns and tree planting projects. Volunteers perform valuable duties at recycling programs and humane society centers, and they have opportunities to meet people with experience in ecology. They are able to share information and ideas.

Nature Centers: Nature centers sponsor programs so that people can experience first-hand what they are learning. Nature centers encourage the public to become more sensitive to the environment through nature hikes, canoe trips, film festivals, and various educational demonstrations.

Membership in an Environmental Group: A wide variety of environmental organizations exist on local, state, and national levels. Many groups offer special programs for high schools and colleges. The Student Environmental Action Coalition (SEAC) has a list of national programs young adults can get involved in. (See Resources for further details.)

Many educational facilities are networking or joining forces with national environmental groups and community programs to form a coalition for activism. The Izaak Walton League of America has a stream-monitoring program for high school and college students. Educators, local environmentalists, and students monitor the health of streams and identify sources of water pollution and soil erosion. If pollution is detected, students get involved in environmental activism.

An important benefit of hands-on learning is carried on in the students' family life. Students bring their enthusiasm home, encouraging families to recycle, save energy resources, care for pets more humanely, and get involved in other ecology activities. This is truly eco-values coming alive in our society in a very positive way!

The environmental crisis of the twentieth century is a result of humankind's crisis in values. For a variety of historical reasons, society has lost sight of the fact that planet earth, as well as the universe, belongs to the divine creator.

Instead we have turned nature into a commodity to satisfy our own appetites, regardless of the effects on the earth's health. One way out of this mess is to honestly come to terms with our values and relationship with the divine creator. In this process we are able to rethink our lifestyles, priorities, and ecological values. This is where eco-value strategies come into play.

Learn About the Environment	STOP for a moment and ask yourself: How are you acquiring knowledge about ecology and earth care skills? Reading environmental literature? Talking to others who have an interest in ecology? Participating in an environmental group? There are many different ways to learn. The Resources section of this book may give you additional ideas about activism.

SCRIPTURE-SPEAK

"Behold, I make all things new" (Rev 21:5).

"According to the commission of God given to me, like a skilled master builder, I laid a foundation and another man is building upon it" (1Cor 3:10).

Part Two
Eco-Value Strategies

*"Until he extends his circle of compassion to all living things,
man will not himself find peace."*
—*Albert Schweitzer*

How To Discover Personal Values

Let me ask you a couple of questions. In the morning do you brush your teeth and comb your hair? Which values motivate you to do these things?

You are probably more aware of your daily habits—like combing your hair—than how you value good hygiene. We go about doing all sorts of things—eating, having fun, studying, and getting together with friends—without thinking about our values. But our values consciously and unconsciously guide our thoughts and actions. Sometimes, though, we confront a situation that forces us to stop and think about our values and what is most important to us.

I have a friend, Tina, who juggles a busy schedule of school, studies, a part-time job, and social activities. (Can you guess that she values high achievement?) Tina is always on the go, so she tries to save time whenever possible. For a while, Tina got into the habit of running to a fast food restaurant and ordering a cheeseburger, fries, and a cold drink. She values the convenience. One day Tina read a report on factory farming. She was shocked to learn how animals are given chemicals for rapid weight gain and bred in unhealthy conditions. She reevaluated how she valued the convenience of a fast food diet.

We can lean how to identify our values and the importance they play in our lives. The strategies which help us to know our values are called *value clarification* techniques. Value clarification is a clear, step-by-step approach to knowing one's values. In this section, we will use strategies, questions, and other methods that will allow you to explore and discover your personal values.

How will you do this? You will use a step-by-step guide that provides the following:

Information—facts and knowledge you'll need to increase your understanding of value systems. The information is described in non-technical language.

Process—strategies, games, and exercises to help you discover and appreciate your ecological values or eco-values.

Action—suggested ideas to put your eco-values to work in your daily life.

Each strategy is designed to provide opportunities to see how your values influence your choices and priorities, and what is important to you. You will be able to answer the following questions:

- What are my ecological values?
- What significance do these values play in my daily life?
- How do they influence how I treat nature?

Of course you will not automatically answer these questions. It takes time to understand one's values. But as you try to answer these questions, your real ecological values will become clear.

To help you with this questioning process, I would strongly recommend that you keep a Values Journal. A small, pocket-size notebook will do. Journaling helps you to collect your private thoughts and ideas. It doesn't matter if you keep a daily journal. Each of you will decide how often it is necessary to jot down your insights and ideas. The important thing is to actively collect your thoughts as they occur.

A word of caution: Understanding our eco-values is part of a long journey. Avoid rushing down the road! Take time to read, sort things out, talk with family and friends, and complete each value clarification strategy. Remember how we said this is like learning the words of a new song? Take time to enjoy the music!

Happy reading . . . exploring . . . and learning!

Personal Value System

A value is a standard, belief, or ethical principle which is held in high esteem and acted upon.

STOP and reflect on several time-honored values in our society:

Independence	Happiness
Achievement	Courage
Work	Privacy
Generosity	Thrift
Decency	Prosperity

These values are intertwined in the American psyche, heritage, and culture. To a greater or lesser extent each one may be part of your personal values depending on your beliefs, priorities, and lifestyle. And to some degree they may compliment or conflict with your earth-conscious values. This is something you will be sorting out in this book.

In this section we will explore the nature of values, as well as clarify your Personal Value System and its importance to ecology.

Information   We acquire a whole collection of values from our culture,
                       ethnic and family background, community, school and edu-
                       cational experiences, religion, and civic organizations. Dur-
                       ing our formative years we sort through these values and
                       over time—even into adulthood—we develop a Personal
                       Value System (PVS).

                              Our Personal Value System is made up of virtues, be-
                       liefs, and standards or ethics of right and wrong. The PVS
                       shapes how we view ourselves, family relationships, friend-
                       ships, leisure time, the global community, and nature.

Process   To understand what *you* value, STOP and observe your
                       daily habits. Ask yourself the following questions:

Personal Appearance

How important is physical appearance to you?
Do you judge people by their personal appearance?
Does your appearance reflect how you feel about yourself?

Health Habits

Do you exercise regularly?
Do you eat a balanced diet?
Do you care about personal hygiene?

Financial Spending Habits

Are you a "saver" or a "spender"?
Are you saving money for a goal?
Are you offended when someone asks to borrow money from you?

Shopping Habits

Where do you shop?
Do you buy the first item you see, or do you carefully select your purchase?
Do you look for sales?

Achievement

What are your accomplishments?
What are you proud of?
Do you set goals for yourself?
Do you set your sights high or low?

Choice of Friends

How do you choose your friends?
What do you look for in a friend?
Are you a friend?
Would your friends describe you as a "giver," "receiver," or both?

Outlook on Life

Do you look on the positive, bright side of life, or do you look at the negative, gloomy side?
Are you curious about life?
Do you have a sense of adventure?
Do you enjoy a sense of humor?

Environmental Interests

Are you aware of the real dangers of pollution on the environment?
Do you do something daily to help support a healthy environment?
Do you belong to an environmental group or club?

STOP and think about your answers and values. List five things you value most in life.

1. _____

2. _____

3. _____

4. _____

5. _____

As you look at your values, are they clear? Can you name them, or are they somewhat vague? Is is difficult to list or describe some of your values? At this point do not worry if some of your values are not clear. Some might even seem fuzzy. It is normal to feel even puzzled. As you take steps with each eco-value exercise, the picture of your personal values will become complete and whole.

Action   Make an agreement with yourself that you will take the necessary time and effort to know your ecological values.

Repeat the following:

I, _____, believe that values are very important and guide how I treat myself, my neighbor, my relationship with God and nature. I will make a *commitment* to understanding my values.

Importance of Your PVS ————————————————

Information   Your values shape your personality and identity. Personal values tell you and the rest of the world *who* you are and what you *believe* in.

STOP for a moment and imagine yourself standing in front of a small group of trusted friends. Let's suppose they are going to describe you as a person. What would they say? Would they say you are a leader? friendly? enthusiastic? dependable? loyal? creative? Examine your personal characteristics. How do they reveal your deeper values?

Now take a look at your choice of clothes, how you style your hair, and your outside interests. This is all part of your identity. Your value system guides your choices, decisions, and what is important to you.

Your Personal Value System gives your life meaning, purpose, and direction. What do you want out of life? What is your philosophy of life? Are you an optimist? Optimists look at the positive side of things. Are you a pragmatist? Pragmatists look at things in down to earth and practical ways. Are you hopeful about the future of our environment? Your Personal Value System helps you to answer these questions.

You acquire the majority of your values from your family. Certain values are handed down from generation to generation. You have heard the expressions "Like father, like son" and "Like mother, like daughter." You and your family are part of a family history and wider circle of relatives. Your family has membership in a church and community. You and your family are also part of the natural world. So your values connect you to family, friends, neighbors, strangers, and all living species. This is called the *web of life*. Like a giant spider web, all life is connected together. The web remains either strong or weak depending on how we treat it.

Process   Explore how your values give your life purpose and direction. What do you want out of life? What are your personal
goals? List three goals that are most important to you.

1. _____

2. _____

3. _____

Explore how your values shape your identity—who you are
as a person. Remember how you imagined a group of
friends describing you. What three words would they use to
describe you best?

1. _____ 2. _____ 3. _____

Now look a little deeper at your identity. How do these three
words reveal your personal values? Example: If you are
described as "friendly," do you value helping others?

_____

_____

_____

Action   Think about what you have discovered about yourself and
your values in the above exercise. How do your values connect you to the web of life? Example: If you are described as
a "leader," do you get involved in environmental activities?
Do you speak up when you see an environmental problem?
Think about ways you can use your strengths and characteristics to be more involved in the world around you.

Identifying "Silent" Values ———————————————

Information

We communicate our values through our actions and behavior. "Actions speak louder than words" is a true observation about human behavior and values.

Some of our deeper values are revealed in small, less obvious ways. It is sometimes difficult to recognize these values because they are not always obvious in our everyday actions and behavior. Nevertheless, they quietly exist within our value system. Some of our deeper ecological values lie here.

My daughter has a friend, Anne, who feels a deep compassion for animals. Anne's brother is allergic to animal fur, so their family does not have any pets. Anne has few opportunities to show her compassion toward animals. One day there was a news story about suspected animal cruelty at a local pet shop. Anne was outraged! She visited the pet shop and protested the injustice to the store owner. Anne's friends were surprised at her actions. Some knew that she was fond of animals, but they didn't know she cared so deeply.

We can identify our unconscious or seemingly silent ecological values through a strategy called free association. In free association we report the *first thought* that comes to mind in response to a given word or incomplete sentence. Free association allows us to reach into our inner thoughts and values and bring them to the surface. Sometimes you are surprised to discover some of your deeper values.

Process

In order to identify your unconscious ecological values, complete the following sentences. Read each sentence and write down the *first* thought that comes to mind.

To me, the earth is _____

Our environmental crisis has _____

The earth would be beautiful if _____

God's creation is _____

I experience God's presence _____

I feel sad _____

Pollution does _____

We can help save _____

I hope _____

If only people could _____

Animals have the right _____

Nature has _____

When I am alone with nature _____

Litter should _____

If animals could talk _____

I get angry _____

We should protest _____

To help save energy _____

To show compassion _____

I care _____

Action   What did you freely reveal about your inner thoughts and unconscious values? What are you learning about your deeper ecological values?

_____

_____

_____

PVS and Nature-Oriented Values ————————————————

Information   Within your Personal Value System are different nature-oriented values which give you a sensitivity to the world's ecosystems. Nature-oriented values guide your appreciation of the physical universe as well as the earth's land, water, plant species, and wildlife. We open our eyes and ears to nature. We pause for a moment to enjoy a beautiful sunset or to listen to a songbird. A walk in the woods can be both pleasurable and refreshing. Nature-oriented values also compel us to be more respectful of the environment. This encourages us to feel closer to nature.

Aesthetic Nature Values
Aesthetic means responsive to and appreciative of beauty. Our aesthetic nature values deal with the wonder and beauty of creation. We enjoy magnificent scenery. Aesthetic nature values help open our five senses to the physical world around us. We delight in the fresh smell of spring flowers or the crisp air after a new snow. Our imagination is also stimulated. We gaze at clouds and imagine them to be funny or strange creatures. Aesthetic values enrich the human spirit.

These values are captured in art, poetry, music, and photography. Many individuals have a hobby that involves nature and aesthetic values. Wildlife photography is one example.

People enjoy watching waterfalls. Flowing water is mystical and enchanting. Ansel Adams, the legendary nature photographer, had a special talent for capturing the aesthetic qualities of spectacular waterfalls in his photo art.

Character-Building Values

Wildlands provide opportunities for endurance and to learn how to care about our physical condition. Through outdoor activities we learn patience, cooperation, and endurance. Camping in the wilds with a group teaches cooperation. Backpacking along a wooded trail builds our physical stamina and teaches us to respect the ruggedness of nature.

Character-building values encourage good stewardship. Cooperation and team work are needed in clean up campaigns.

Preservation Values

Humans are historical beings. We record and preserve our history through art, literature, and historical monuments. We preserve national forests and parks for natural historical, recreational, and cultural use. Natural areas, like Death Valley, are preserved for their outstanding beauty. Historical areas include birthplaces of presidents, famous battlefields and forts, and ancient Indian ruins. Recreational areas provide outstanding water and land resources for outdoor activities. Cultural areas provide attractive settings for the enjoyment of fine arts performances.

Recreational Values

These values promote responsible use of the great outdoors for recreation and relaxation. Humans enjoy watching wildlife, viewing landscapes, climbing mountains, and hiking forest trails. Humans interact with nature in order to relax, appreciate the outdoors, and recreate one's physical, emotional, and spiritual well-being. Lately, stewardship values have become associated with recreational values. We are more aware of how our recreational activities impact the environment. Evaluating how off-road motor vehicles can tear up fragile terrains is an example of this. Many states have passed tough laws restricting off-road vehicles to designated trails.

Utilitarian Values

Utilitarian relates to engaging in activities that bring the greatest good or happiness to the greatest number of people. This belief system says that humans have an obligation to care for nature for humanity's sake. We should preserve and wisely use the earth's resources in order to guarantee that future generations will have sufficient natural resources. Energy conservation is one example of utilitarian values. Reducing oil consumption and finding alternative energy sources will help future generations have sufficient resources.

Utilitarian values stress the need to take care of the earth or else humanity will perish. Certainly these values become stronger as we experience the grave problems of global warming and severe droughts.

Process   Answer the following questions and observe how nature-oriented values are a part of your Personal Value System.

Aesthetic Nature Values

Do you take nature walks?
Do you have a hobby that captures the beauty and value of nature?
Do you enjoy the peace and solitude of nature?

Character-Building Values

Do you enjoy camping, hiking, or backpacking?
Do you build personal strengths like patience, endurance, and cooperation through out-of-door activities?

Preservation Values

Do you visit national parks and historical museums?
Do you enjoy learning about our country's heritage and culture?

Recreational Values

Are you conscious of how your recreational activities impact nature?
Do you obey conservation and anti-littering laws?

Utilitarian Values

Do you try to help conserve energy?
Do you recycle to reduce waste in landfills so that there will be available land for future generations?
Do you use alternative forms of transportation?

Action   Go for a walk each day for a week and observe the air, natural environment, and flying and crawling creatures. As you walk, reflect on one nature-oriented value you hold in high priority. See how it enriches your relationship with the earth.

Spiritual Ecological Values

Information   Spiritual ecological values connect us to God and all of God's creation. We acknowledge that God is the author of creation (Ps 8:1).

Spiritual eco-values are different from nature-oriented values. The latter guide us to appreciate the beauty of nature. Spiritual eco-values motivate us to become more deeply involved in God's creation. We confront our responsibilities in caring about nature. As Christians we are called to serve God. The book of Daniel says: "People of every language serve him" (Dan 7:14).

In order to serve God and care about the environment, we must discipline our appetites and consumer habits. Spiritual ecological values help us to restrain human impulses to exploit nature. Greed and selfishness destroy the environment. Spiritual eco-values guide our daily choices and decisions about how we use the earth's resources.

Spiritual ecological values help strengthen our connection in the web of life. We deepen our commitment to protect and preserve life. There are three spiritual eco-values: creation values, reverence for life values, and stewardship values.

Creation Values

Creation values motivate us to acknowledge that the divine creator owns the earth. The book of Genesis tells us that God created the heavens and the earth (Gen 1:1-2). The creator looked at everything he had made and found it very good (Gen 1:31).

When we acknowledge that God reigns over the universe, we search for our rightful place on earth. In the Old Testament we learn that we are tenants or residents in God's house, the earth (Lev 25:23).

Creation values move us to be awed and humbled by magnificent sunsets, midnight skies, and vast oceans. These values inspire us to worship God, the author of all creation.

Reverence for Life Values

Reverence for life values embraces a love for life. These values expand the commandment of love to include love of God, fellow human beings, and creatures great and small. We are concerned about the welfare of all God's species.

Albert Schweitzer reminded us that every creature has a special place on earth and a right to that place. He believed that when humans show a reverence for life they do not act superior to God's creatures. Rather humans show empathy and compassion for all species. We abhor any brutality to God's creatures. When the world learned that elephants were being slaughtered by greedy poachers, people were moved by compassion to protest the abuse. Our creator has commanded us to preserve all species and rescue them from destruction (Gen 6:11-9:17).

Stewardship Values

Stewardship describes our responsibility to manage the earth's resources wisely. We are reminded that God owns the universe. Stewardship values move us to actively care for the earth. We are dependent on a healthy environment, and it is our obligation to preserve nature. The book of

Genesis shows us that we are to guard and protect the earth (Gen 2:15). We are good stewards when we recycle, avoid littering, reduce food waste, and help save energy.

"The earth is the Lord's and the fullness thereof" (Ps 24:1). This psalm beautifully captures the Christian concept of stewardship of the earth. The earth is God's creation, and we are to watch over it, as good stewards, for as long as the Lord has dominion over us.

Process

Creation Values

How do you give praise and glory to the divine creator?
How do you acknowledge that God reigns over the heavens and earth?
Do you boycott industries that exploit or damage the environment?

Reverence for Life Values

Do you avoid purchasing products that are harmful to marine mammals and wildlife?
How do you show compassion for animals?
What do you do when you see cruelty to animals?

Stewardship Values

Are you conscious of how you use daily water supplies?
Do you support an environmental group?

Action   In your Values Journal reflect on the biblical verse: "It is required of stewards that they be found trustworthy" (1 Cor 4:2). Describe how you are learning about what it means to be a good steward in God's creation. How are you fulfilling your responsibilities to care for the earth?

Ecological Enterprise ————————————————————

Information   Our Personal Value System can provide a satisfying philosophy of life. Certain values offer a heightened positive responsiveness to creation, the global community and all living species. This involves an enlarged sense of responsibility and being involved in what is called the *ecological enterprise*. The ecological enterprise embraces a powerful love of life. It is stewardship in action! This includes the ability to give love in one's family, to be actively concerned about one's neighbor and the welfare of society, and contribute to the growth and protection of nature. The ecological enterprise looks beyond the circle of family and friends and embraces a large community.

Process   Reflect on your sense of responsibility to your family, neighbor, society, global community, animals, and nature.

What is your responsibility to your family? How do you show love to those closest to you? How do you extend this love to strangers?

_____

_____

_____

_____

What is your responsibility to society? Your local community? How do your learn about problems in your community?

_____

_____

_____

_____

Pollution does not respect geographic boundaries. Waste and toxic chemicals can travel the globe via water ecosystems. What is your responsibility to the global community? Are you concerned about poverty in the third world?

_____

_____

_____

_____

Action   In your Values Journal reflect on the biblical verse: "Ever since the creation of the world, his invisible nature has been clearly perceived in the things that have been made" (Rom 1:20). How do you deepen your love of God as you become closer to other people and nature?

PVS and the Family Tree ————————————————

Information   Your family background is weighted with ethnic traditions, rit-
                     uals, customs, and beliefs about nature. Your family tree has
                     deep roots in cultural values and attitudes about the earth as
                     well as in generations of family values. A family that has migrat-
                     ed from a rural setting to urban life may cherish a kinship with
                     the earth. From generation to generation entrenched atti-
                     tudes and beliefs about nature get passed along.

Process   Identify the experiences and family members who influ-
                     enced your sensitivity to nature.

Describe your father's attitude toward nature and ecology.

——

——

Describe your mother's attitude toward nature and ecology.

_____

_____

Describe a relative you admired who showed a special interest in nature.

_____

_____

Parental attitudes can influence us. How did your parents react to:

• a child's wanting a pet? _____

_____

• news stories about pollution? _____

_____

• politicians wanting to safeguard the environment? _____

_____

• Earth Day events (or similar activities)? _____

_____

• anti-litter campaigns? _____

_____

• reports about endangered species? _____

_____

Which of the following did your family provide opportunities for?
(Check all that apply.)

_____ camping   _____ hiking

_____ planting flowers   _____ planting trees

_____ beachcombing   _____ seashell collecting

_____ bird watching   _____ exploring caves

_____ bicycle trips   _____ planting a garden

_____ travel to state or national parks

_____ other outdoor activities (please specify)

_____

_____

What can you recall about these experiences? _____

_____

What are your favorite memories? _____

_____

Think about your immediate family experiences. Write the first thing that comes
to mind as you complete each sentence.

In my family, nature is _____

_____

In my family, animals are _____

_____

In my family, curiosity and asking questions are _____

_____

In my family, boys are allowed _____

_____

In my family, girls are allowed _____

_____

In my family, nature education _____

_____

Action　　　　　Talk with family members who share nature-oriented values.

How do they view the environment? How do they enjoy nature? How do they express their values? What new opportunities are open to you to act on your values?

_____

_____

_____

_____

In your Values Journal reflect on the biblical verse: "I will give you shepherds after my own heart, who will feed you with knowledge and understanding" (Jer 3:15).

PVS and Education ———————————————————

Information   Your schooling and educational experiences have greatly
                       influenced your thinking, ethical standards, personal phi-
                       losophy, and eco-values. A certain teacher, biology class,
                       field trip, or book may have left a deep impression. You
                       might recall a teacher who stimulated your curiosity in
                       nature, wildlife, or the natural sciences. Perhaps this
                       teacher encouraged you to begin valuing and appreciating
                       life in a special way.

Process   Identify the educational experiences that have helped
                       shape your love of nature or interest in ecology.

Describe a teacher who encouraged interest in the natural world.

_____

_____

_____

Did this teacher influence your philosophy of life? If so, how?

_____

_____

_____

Did the teacher help you to see life differently? If so, in what way?

_____

_____

_____

Describe a favorite subject that stimulated your curiosity about ecology or the environmental crisis.

_____

_____

_____

Write down other positive educational experiences that contributed to your appreciation of nature.

_____

_____

_____

Action   Education is ongoing. Today, how do you increase your knowledge about ecology? Reading? Talking to others who are interested in nature? Watching TV programs about the environment?

_____

_____

_____

_____

In your Values Journal reflect on the biblical verse: "The wise man also may hear and increase in learning" (Prov 1:5).

Religion and Nature Values ———————————————

Information   A family's religious practices are often a training ground
                  for teaching right and wrong, morality, social responsibility,
                  and environmental ethics. We learn about how to respect
                  God's creation through our parents' example and actions
                  and their religious beliefs about creation.

     In families where there is a high regard for preserving
nature, God is seen as love. Children are encouraged to
experience God's love. They are taught that God created all
things good. Parents provide opportunities for children to
plant flowers or a garden, raise pets, respect wildlife, and
appreciate God's goodness. In worship and song children
grow in their understanding of God's love and creation.
They develop ecological values which guide their choices
and decisions about how to use the earth's resources wisely.

Process

Worship

Observe how many hymns and songs that you sing at church include references
to creation and nature.

Notice the psalms that are used in daily worship. Reflect on the psalms that call
us to serve God and to preserve and protect nature.

Celebration

Does your parish honor the feast of St. Francis of Assisi? Many congregations have a special liturgy showing respect for ecology.

Does your family celebrate the seasons of the year in special ways? Do these celebrations give you a sense of appreciation for the awe and wonder of life?

Environmental Ethics

How did your parents expect you to treat nature? How did they teach you to observe conservation laws or humane treatment of wildlife?

Did you belong to a church club or attend a camp? Did it add to your understanding and respect for creation? Did it stimulate your curiosity about God, ethics (right and wrong), nature, and purpose in life?

Action

Does your parish sponsor environmental activities? If not, can you suggest any ideas or activities?

_____

_____

_____

_____

In your Values Journal think about the biblical verse: "You did show me the path of life; in your presence there is fullness of joy" (Ps 16:11). Faith is a celebration of God's love and joy. Discover positive experiences at your church or within your family to deepen your love for God's creation.

Acting on Real Values

In saying that we act on our real values, the key words are *act* and *real.*

Most Americans would say they value reducing waste. No one wants our valuable land resources gobbled up by a glut of garbage and trash. Yet, surprisingly, only a fraction of our public actually practices the three Rs of waste reduction: Reduce, Reuse, and Recycle. Many communities still do not place a high priority on participating in recycling programs or encourage citizens to purchase goods made from recycled materials. Hence, while a majority of Americans may agree that recycling is worthwhile (ideal value), only a portion of the public puts this into practice (real value).

We need to clarify and think about our actual values— those we are willing to commit to. Once again, if we are going to persist with a meaningful environmental movement, then we need to know our real values and act on them.

In this section, you will examine your real values, identify specific (real) eco-values, and understand how you are committed to them.

Eco-Value Clarification ——————————————————

Information   Are your values and beliefs *consistent* with your intentions, words, and actions? Are some of your real eco-values still vague or fuzzy?

To help sort out the answers to these questions, you can participate in an eco-value clarification exercise. Eco-value clarification is a strategy that helps to clarify personal values and to point out inconsistencies. At the end of this exercise you will be able to determine the content and power of the eco-values in your Personal Value System.

Process   The directions are simple. Circle one of the codes. Y for Yes, N for No, and M for Maybe. Begin by asking yourself:

Am I someone who:

1. is capable of handling opinions different from my own?   Y   N   M

2. wonders about the future of our environment?   Y   N   M

3. feels hopeful about the future?   Y   N   M

4. is conscientious about saving fuel and energy?   Y   N   M

5. believes nature is a place to "know thyself"?   Y   N   M

6. believes animals have a place in nature and a right to that place?   Y   N   M

7. believes we are accountable to a divine creator for our treatment of nature?   Y   N   M

8. is willing to share the earth with other creatures?   Y   N   M

9. practices recycling?   Y   N   M

10. reuses household materials or goods when possible?   Y   N   M

11. recognizes that nature is a beautiful part of God's kingdom?   Y   N   M

12. acknowledges that the wilderness is a habitat for other
    species to grow and live?   Y   N   M

13. believes that we should locate and construct buildings
    and highways with the good of other species in mind?   Y   N   M

14. is sensitive to nature's beauty?   Y   N   M

15. will crusade for environmental causes?   Y   N   M

16. will write letters to politicians and officials regarding
    environmental problems?   Y   N   M

17. feels obliged to fight for the rights of animals?   Y   N   M

18. will participate in anti-litter and clean-up campaigns?   Y   N   M

19. will participate in a peace vigil?   Y   N   M

20. will actively support a community beautification project? Y   N   M

21. believes in hunting animals for sport?   Y   N   M

22. will join and support an environmental group?   Y   N   M

23. believes non-violence is achievable?   Y   N   M

24. purchases environmentally friendly or safe products?   Y   N   M

25. will participate in a boycott of companies that produce
    hazardous waste?   Y   N   M

26. likes to take over leadership responsibilities?   Y   N   M

27. needs to buy new clothes every season?   Y   N   M

28. likes to volunteer for jobs on a committee?   Y   N   M

29. would die for my beliefs and values?   Y   N   M

30. has high ethical standards of right and wrong?   Y   N   M

31. buys health foods from health food stores?   Y   N   M

32. tries to understand and respect other opinions?   Y   N   M

33. believes conservation laws need strict enforcement?   Y   N   M

34. responds with compassion when animals suffer cruelty? Y   N   M

Review your responses. Especially note your Yes answers.

What are you learning about your Personal Value System? How do your responses reflect your real eco-values?

_____

_____

_____

Action   Just for today: Commit yourself to acting on one eco-value
                    that is *emerging* in your Personal Value System. How can you
                    act on this value?

                    In your Values Journal reflect on the biblical verse: "Each of
                    us shall give account of himself to God" (Rom 14:12).

Turning Point ──────────────────────────────────

Information   Our relationship with the earth can be influenced by significant turning points. These are dramatic events which stir
our emotions and affect our decisions, values, and changes
in behavior. A good example of this was seen during the
scorching summer of 1988. Many people began to worry
about the greenhouse effect. They became acutely aware of
how their lifestyles were contributing to global warming,
and they made conscious modifications in their daily living
and consumer habits. People were more aware of the need
to purchase fuel-efficient cars and trucks.

Turning points may include witnessing a natural disas-
ter (flood, drought, forest fire, etc.) or man-made catastro-
phe (oil spill, poison gas leak, etc.) For many people,
seeing a television documentary on the destruction of rainforests or how our oceans are poisoned may jar their sensi-
tivities. But the reaction is more than "oh-my-gosh." The
emotions are stirred and positive action follows. A person's
real eco-values are challenged and put into motion. The
individual wants to take positive action to help save the
earth.

Process   Ecologists can point to turning point events in their lives
                         which affected their real eco-values. Think about occur-
                         rences which have jarred your earth-sensitive values and
                         influenced how you treat nature.

Recall and describe a significant turning point experience. What happened?

_____

_____

_____

How did this turning point experience stir you to some type of action? What
decisions did you make?

_____

_____

_____

_____

Action   Turning point events challenge our *real* eco-values.

Describe your personal eco-values which have been called to action. Do you feel
more compassion for wildlife? Are you changing your buying or consumer
habits? Are you involved in an awareness campaign to bring attention to the
environmental problem?

_____

_____

_____

_____

PVS and Commitment

Information   We act on eco-values which are held in high regard. Such behavior requires a personal *commitment*. When we commit ourselves to something we act with conviction, and this involves investing personal time, planning, and exerting energy. Consider the following:

Conviction is the strong belief in one or more personal eco-values.

Action involves how a person follows through on personal beliefs and values. This is the legwork, so to speak.

Time entails the hours devoted to planning and action.

Energy involves the mental, physical, emotional, and spiritual intensity expended to fulfill one's commitments.

Process   Reflect on your personal commitment to ecology as you complete this exercise. Focus on one environmental problem or issue you are concerned about.

Describe the environmental problem.

_____

_____

_____

_____

How do you respond to the issue or problem with personal conviction? Do you talk about the problem? Have you tried to bring this problem to someone's attention?

_____

_____

_____

_____

How much time do you devote to this concern? Have you tried to deal with this problem within the past month or year?

_____

_____

_____

_____

Action   In your Values Journal reflect on Thoreau's observation: "What is the use of a house if you don't have a decent planet to put it on?" How does Thoreau's question tie into the discussion on making a commitment? How does he show us that we must act on our ecological values with firm conviction? What will happen if we don't?

Action

Action may be defined as: (1) an act of will; (2) a type of behavior or deed; (3) a process that involves more than one step or is capable of repetition.

ACTION speaks louder than words.

ACTION shows what we believe in.

ACTION puts our real values in motion.

ACTION is energy.

ACTION says: "This is what I am committed to" and sets up a game plan for follow-through.

Now let's see how you *practice* your eco-values and explore daily habits which reflect your values.

Values in Motion ————————————————————

Information   Value actualization begins with a person *searching* for values, *identifying* values, *choosing* personal values and ultimately *practicing* values. A person's values are in motion! They become an important part of our daily lives.

Process

Check the ecological actions that you are doing or plan to do in the near future.

_____ use energy-efficient appliances, including VCRs, radios

_____ carpool when possible

_____ ride a bicycle or walk instead of driving when possible

_____ buy products that can be reused or recycled

_____ donate used clothing, furniture, appliances for reuse

_____ plant a tree(s) or other regreening activities

_____ support conservation laws

_____ recycle glass, used motor oil, plastics, paper

_____ compost yard waste and other disposed material

_____ join an environmental group

_____ write letters to elected officials regarding pollution

_____ participate in a food co-op, if possible

_____ support anti-litter laws

_____ participate in a community garden

_____ use energy-efficient lighting

_____ protest violations of animal rights

_____ participate in community beautification projects

_____ plan ahead to consolidate errands with the car

_____ voice concern about endangered animals

_____ donate time and/or money to an environmental cause

_____ boycott products produced or caught in a harmful way

_____ write letters to companies about your environmental concerns

_____ contact local media about environmental problems

_____ support a local nature center

_____ help organize a neighborhood beautification project

_____ adopt an endangered or protected animal at a zoo or through an environmental group

How much personal *time* and *energy* do you plan to devote to your ecological actions? Circle the ones you are willing to do on a daily or weekly basis.

Action   Examine the ecological action you checked. These are very important in your eco-value system. Include them in your Values Journal as you heighten your awareness of environmental action.

Sacrifice and Change ——————————————————————

Information   Our environmental problems have reached a crisis that confronts our willingness to change our wasteful habits. We have to keep changing how we treat the environment. But what sacrifices are we willing to make? How will we tolerate any inconveniences as we change our lifestyles? People who refuse to change remain passive. They will not make sacrifices to change wasteful habits that contribute to pollution. Each of us must be honest about our willingness to change.

Process

Complete each sentence by writing the first thought that comes to mind.

I will preserve _____

_____

I will protest _____

_____

I will sacrifice _____

_____

I will save _____

_____

I will defend _____

_____

I will conserve _____

_____

I will reuse _____

_____

Action   In your Values Journal reflect on the biblical verse: "All the earth shall be filled with the glory of the Lord" (Num 14:21). The Creator has given us the skills to overcome the problems of pollution. Ask the Creator for help to overcome the passivity that sometimes makes it difficult for us to confront environmental problems.

Feed the Hungry

Information   Hunger is a difficult social and environmental issue for an abundant and consumer-oriented society to confront and effectively remedy.

We often react to the poor and hungry on an emotional level. People respond compassionately with their checkbooks to photos of starving children. Offering money is the most tangible thing to do. Yet most giving people would be surprised to learn that checkbook generosity is not the answer to solving local and global hunger.

Within the past decade, environmental groups and interfaith church councils have learned the wisdom of networking to solve problems of homelessness, social and economic injustice, hunger, and health care. Networking is sharing ideas and resources. People from all disciplines and walks of life—social scientists, farmers, ecologists, politicians, clergy, health care providers, and economists—play crucial roles in confronting these social and global ills. The future of our global community rests on the commitment of these networking activities.

The problems of hunger are complex. The economic, social, political and ecological realities associated with hunger are beyond the scope of this book. Readers are encouraged to get a copy of *How To Make the World a Better*

Place by Jeffrey Hollender (see Resources) to gain an in-depth understanding of local and global hunger issues.

Families can take three important steps to help reduce hunger on local and global levels.

- *Volunteer*

  Find out what is being done in your local community and church to help provide food for the hungry. Is there a soup kitchen? Food bank? Does it need volunteers? Can you donate kitchen equipment and/or food?

- *Network*

  Get involved in a community group, interfaith council, or environmental group that addresses hunger. Get on the mailing list and communicate with others interested in creating positive change.

- *Support Share Our Strength*

  When possible, support the Share Our Strength (SOS) project when you eat out. SOS is an organization of chefs and restauranteurs dedicated to fighting hunger. You can support restaurants that display the SOS logo or you can obtain a free list of SOS members by writing to Share Our Strength, 733 15th Street, N.W., Suite 700, Washington, DC 20005.

Process   As a family, discuss the problem of hunger on a local and global scale.

How do you and family members react to hunger in your community?

_____

_____

_____

How is your church and community addressing hunger?

_____

_____

_____

Action   Read Matthew 19:16.

How does Christ discuss social responsibility? Reflect on Christ's expectations for fulfilling the will of the Father.

_____

_____

_____

Look at ways you can help eliminate hunger in your community. Check with your local church and food bank on volunteer opportunities.

In your Values Journal reflect on the biblical verse: "He who is kind to the poor lends to the Lord, and He will repay him for his deed" (Prov 19:17).

Passing It On

Up to now we have discussed how we acquire our ecological values. We have explored your Personal Values System which includes eco-values. Your eco-values guide your choices about environmental action.

It is important to recognize that your environmental action does not operate in a vacuum. Remember that we learn our real values best from our grandparents, parents, and relatives. Our values are rooted in our family tree and are passed on in its branches and new buds of life. Many of our cherished values are grounded in our Christian faith. "I am the vine, you are the branches," said the Lord (Jn 15:5).

This is similar to the wisdom of native Americans. In the Indian culture children were taught that the ground beneath their feet was the ashes of their ancestors. The children would respect the earth because the land was rich

with the lives of their kin. Children learned how to respect and preserve the earth.

Every generation has an obligation to think of the needs of the next generation. *We work to protect the earth not only for our use but to preserve it and pass it along to our children's children.* Families can provide a variety of opportunities for each member to express his or her ecological values, participate in environmental activities, and do positive things to protect and preserve nature. One vital way to preserve the earth is to become a family of peacemakers. Striving to build loving and peaceful relationships in one's family and community, as well as in the global community, helps to ensure that the life of all species is protected from harm.

Let's discuss specific ways in which families can participate in ecology and how eco-values can guide family decisions and activities.

Environmental Action and Family Life ——————————

Information

Listed below are four ways in which families can share responsibility for environmental action in the home and community. These are suggested ideas. Your family may decide on other activities and is encouraged to do so.

Discuss Issues

Families can become intensely interested in environmental issues that may affect their future. Acid rain, ozone depletion, global warming, and poisoned oceans are critical problems that will impact future generations. Family members need to understand that quick-fix solutions are not available. Everyone needs to learn about the complexities of the issues and what can be done to help remedy them. It helps to discuss these problems openly and to share ideas.

Encourage Reading

Many environmental groups and nature centers publish newsletters and other literature. Your family can get on a mailing list. There are excellent books available at bookstores and libraries on environmental topics. Books make a nice gift for Christmas or birthdays. Families can use reading material to stimulate ideas about environmental activities. (See Resources for further details.)

Group Involvement

Join a local environmental organization, conservation club, 4-H group, or community beautification program. In many cities the department of parks and recreation offers ecology programs and classes. (See Resources for other suggested ideas and a list of specific environmental organizations.)

Writing Letters

When you or your family feels strongly about an environmental problem, you can write a letter to public officials.

Our elected representatives need to hear about our concerns. While one letter might not stop our environmental crisis, it will help to show concern!

Where to write:

The Honorable _____
U.S. Senate
Washington, DC 20510

The Honorable _____
U.S. House of Representatives
Washington, DC 20515

The Honorable (Name of President) _____
The White House
Washington, DC 20500

Process

How can you and your family increase an understanding of local, national, and global environmental problems?

Consider the following:

1. Subscribe to an environmental magazine or newsletter.

2. Join an environmental group.

3. Purchase a book like *50 Simple Things You Can Do to Save the Earth* or *Blueprint for a Green Planet.*

(See Resources for other books and ideas.)

How can you encourage your family to "act local, think global"?

Consider the following:

1. Purchase household products that are earth friendly.

2. Use energy wisely.

3. Avoid products that are harmful to the ozone.

4. Use alternative forms of transportation whenever possible.

Action   Hold a family meeting.

Discuss an environmental problem in your neighborhood or community. Decide as a family what you want to do to help remedy the problem.

_____

_____

_____

_____

In your Values Journal reflect on the biblical verse: "A good man leaves an inheritance to his children's children" (Prov 13:22). By helping to respect and preserve nature, you are passing on an inheritance.

Family Celebrations

Information   Jacques Cousteau once observed, "Producing pollution is negative ecology. Preventing it is positive ecology." Families can participate in positive ecology. There are simple things a family can do with celebrations that can help promote positive ecology. Purchasing a bird feeder at Christmas is one example. Planting a tree on Arbor Day is a positive way to celebrate the earth. Sending greeting cards made from recycled paper is positive.

Process   List ways to combine celebrating holidays and being good
to the earth.

1. _____

2. _____

3. _____

Give the earth a family gift. Purchase a live, potted Christmas tree and plant it later or select a new bird house. Other
gifts?

Earth Day
How can you involve your family and friends in an Earth
Day celebration? Earth Day is held "annually" on April 22.
Can you help organize a clean-up campaign? If you can't
think of something today and need time to plan, see Re-
sources for organizations that offer ideas for Earth Day cel-
ebrations. The National Wildlife Federation has special
Earth Day kits.

Family Picnic
Avoid using plastic forks and spoons and throwaway stuff
like styrofoam cups and plates. Purchase a picnic set that is
reusable. Little things don't save the world but they count
and add up.

Action   Have a "Prevent Pollution" jar which collects ideas on how
to prevent pollution. Family members are free to print
ideas on scraps of reusable paper. Once a month an "idea"
is drawn from the jar and is open for discussion and possible action.

Strength in Numbers

Information

There is strength in numbers. This is an important concept for everyone to learn. A group of people—a family, neighbors, and community—committed to an environmental cause can pool their strength, knowledge, and resources. This sharing of ideas is called networking.

We can help each other to understand that when people work together they can solve environmental problems. Groups can get involved in clean-up campaigns, nature festivals, and regreening projects, to name just a few efforts. Organizations like the Regeneration and America the Beautiful Fund are dedicated to improving the quality of the environment and community living. (See Resources for further details.) Children see adult role models and eco-values in action. They broaden their own "people skills" and participation in the ecological enterprise. There is a sense of hope and optimism for the future.

Process

Are there opportunities for your family and friends to participate in neighborhood, community, or coastal clean-up projects? Can you adopt an animal at a local zoo? Can you stop buying products that have been tested on animals? Other ideas?

List one activity that you and your family can agree to do.

_____

_____

_____

_____

As a family, how can you contribute to the idea that there is strength in numbers?

_____

_____

_____

_____

Action

Contact a community-oriented environmental group listed in the Resources section. Follow up on the programs they offer in your community. Or contact a local nature center and inquire about environmental activities it sponsors. Volunteer to help.

_____

_____

As a family, discuss the biblical verse: "Whatever your hands find to do, do with your might" (Eccl 9:10). How has the creator given each family member talents that can be used to make the world a little better?

Peacemakers —————————————————————————

Information

Human conflicts and warfare destroy the earth's ecosystems. War and destructive weapons can disrupt and alter the delicate balance of the environment's life support systems. Nations are armed to the teeth with deadly weapons that inflict massive overkill power and chemical fallout that knows no boundaries. The aftermath from aggression in one corner of the world is not confined to a single geographic region. Sophisticated weapons, stockpiled by even poor third world countries, assault all species of life and destroy the delicate functioning of the planet's ecosystems.

The 1991 Persian Gulf War produced untold human and environmental misery. The "popular little war," as it was called in the U.S. press, was over oil. World leaders were largely indifferent to the environmental damage.

Scientists estimate that the Gulf War's ecological damage will linger for generations. First, there was the devastating oil spill. Iraqi soldiers deliberately opened the valve at Kuwait's Mina al Ahmadi oil depot, pouring millions of barrels of oil into the Persian Gulf. The oil slick covered fragile marine ecosystems. The stakes for Kuwait's oil were high. Next, hundreds of oil wells were sabotaged and set ablaze. The skies over the Middle East blackened as thick clouds of billowing smoke from burning oil wells raged out of control. The fires, thick smoke, soot, and carbon monoxide have impaired climate conditions, desert habitats, and agricultural interests.

Ecologists are called to be peacemakers. Ecologists understand the relationship of conflict between countries and the deadly consequences in the global environment. Peacemakers serve a special role in helping to promote harmony in the human community. In the sermon on the mount, Christ said, "Blest too the peacemakers; they shall be called sons of God" (Mt 5:9).

John Muir understood Christ's command to serve the divine creator loyally for his sake and to abandon self-interest, prejudice, hatred, and greed. Muir was a good steward and peacemaker who valued honest, open communication, negotiation, and forgiveness. He decried those who fostered strife through violence for personal advantage and profit.

St. Francis of Assisi showed us how to be peacemakers. His formula for advancing interpersonal harmony and love is seen in his prayer:

> Lord, make me an instrument of thy peace; where there is hatred, let me sow love; where there is doubt, faith; where there is despair, hope; where there is darkness, light; and where there is sadness, joy. O Divine Master, grant that I may not so much seek to be consoled as to console; to be understood as to understand; to be loved as to love; for it is in giving that we receive, it is in pardoning that we are pardoned, and it is in dying that we are born in eternal life.

Process

How do you value peace? How important is it to get along with others?

_____

_____

_____

_____

Christ talked about love, healing, and building a fellowship on earth: "What I say to you is: everyone who grows angry with his brother shall be liable to judgment" (Mt 5:22).

Reflect on these words of Christ. What do they mean to you?

_____

_____

_____

_____

Christ was tough-minded about what is required to eliminate retaliation in conflict. "You have heard the commandment, 'An eye for an eye, a tooth for a tooth.' But what I say to you is: Offer no resistance to injury" (Mt 5:38). "You have heard 'You shall love your countryman but hate your enemy.' My command to you is: Love your enemies, pray for your persecutors" (Mt 5:43).

What do these commands mean to you?

_____

_____

_____

_____

How do you promote peace in family relationships?

_____

_____

_____

_____

With your neighbor? With a friend?

_____

_____

_____

_____

How do you practice forgiveness when you are hurt?

_____

_____

_____

_____

Action

You can be a peacemaker in your family, with friends, and in your community. A peacemaker desires to promote harmony and repair injured relationships. There are several action steps to consider:

- Check with your church to see what is being done to work for peace. Many churches sponsor peace and human justice activities as well as network with larger, national non-violent organizations.
- Promote non-violence in your family. Take an inventory of "violence" that invades your family. How much of your family television programming is devoted to violent shows? Does your family play with video games that entertain with "war games" that pretend to produce massive annihilation? As a family, talk openly about television, games, and toys that subtly condone vengeance, prejudice, and hostility. Discuss alternative forms of entertainment and leisure time activities that stress nonaggressive behavior.

- Albert Einstein knew the value of peace and justice in the global community. He understood the raw power of destructive weapons and, hence, actively encouraged people to join the War Resisters League, an organization designed to help families promote global peace. Einstein said, "The War Resisters League...is absolutely necessary if humanity is to survive." (Contact: War Resisters League, 339 Lafayette Street, New York, NY 10012; (212) 228-0450. Request to be on their mailing list.)

- Pray for peace. Meditate on the gospel message, "Do not be overcome by evil, but overcome evil with good" (Rom 12:21). As good stewards and pursuers of global justice, we should work to see that everyone, and everything, is protected from the dangers of human aggression. Prayer opens our spirit to find new paths to peace.

Taking Charge!

It seems like more and more environmental problems are hitting news reports. As you learn about them, maybe you have caught yourself saying, "If I were in charge, these things wouldn't happen!" As you hear about a giant corporation polluting a river, maybe you're imagining yourself being in a position of power to confront the corporation's chief executive officer and stockholders. This kind of imaginative problem solving is healthy! It means you are concerned about the fate of the earth, your eco-values have been touched, and you want to respond with action.

In this section, you are given an opportunity to use your imagination and value choices in order to tackle environmental issues. Your friends are invited to participate in these strategies. You will be involved in three value clarification strategies that are designed to help you and others to think about ecological choices, decisions, and actions. Let me explain.

The three value clarification strategies are designed as "games." Each involves describing hypothetical situations that encourage you to clarify your values, take risks, and make choices. With your imagination you will be able to project yourself into the practical situation and picture how you would handle the proposed issues. For example in the strategy *You're the President* you will exercise your "executive powers" to enact legislation that will impact our country, for better or worse! As president of the United States you will sign into law legislation that will affect the economy, environment, powerful special interest groups, and our future. The strategies are both thought-provoking and fun to engage in.

These are group-oriented strategies. They provide opportunities to see how issues, problems, and questions can be addressed from different viewpoints. You can invite your family or friends to participate. Exercises can also be used in ecology clubs or in science and biology classes. They can be used in a variety of home, church, and school settings. Of course you may choose to complete the strategies alone. Aside from the group activities, you may want more private time to think about your choices, ecological values, and action.

A few rules about the games:

1. Allow your imagination to be challenged by the questions in each hypothetical situation.

2. There are no right or wrong answers to the questions. Be open to different opinions and viewpoints.

3. Answer a question as *you* understand it, as it applies to *your values* and beliefs.

One last point. Use your Values Journal to record your reactions to strategies and awareness you are discovering about your eco-values.

Enjoy the strategies! Take charge!

In the News!

Newspapers and TV news document the ill effects of global warming, polluted rivers, foul air, and the like. They also show national environmental groups like Greenpeace, National Audubon Society, and National Wildlife Federation responding to the problems. Sometimes protests are organized, or lawsuits are filed. This prompts grassroots organizations to react on a local level or to participate in the national environmental groups' activism.

Grassroots groups consist of local, interested people from a community. Grassroots movements often rally around a specific environmental cause, like "Save a Wetland" or "Fight Against Radioactive Dumps." Group strength depends on the members' dedication and volunteer spirit. Grassroots groups have to be *selective* about the environmental problems they choose to fight. They cannot save the world. Depending on the size of the groups, and their organizational abilities, grassroots groups can rally around a targeted cause. They can also carefully choose their strategy: organize a protest, sponsor a letter writing campaign, donate money to a national environmental group that is fighting a similar problem, or lead a boycott.

In the News! is a strategy to give you an opportunity to explore your ecological values and *choices* in activism. You have been elected to chair a grassroots group dedicated to fighting problems seen in the news. There is one hitch in this situation. The group consists of good-hearted individuals but is poorly organized. So the group looks to you to make decisions and get things done. Get the picture? O.K., you are ready to start!

Hawk Watch International announced at a recent press conference that "Pets and Stuff," a national chain of pet stores, was selling illegal birds and parrots from foreign countries. The birds were shipped to this country under inhumane conditions. Thousands of birds have suffered diseases and cruel death. There is a "Pets and Stuff" store in your community. The grassroots group believes this is an important problem that the public needs to be aware of. They look to you to lead the cause. What will you do?

Options

1. Organize a protest and encourage the public to boycott the store.

2. Talk to the store manager and try to persuade the manager to stop selling illegal birds.

3. Write to Hawk Watch International for more information about the problem.

4. Other _____

_____

Defenders of Animals issued a document revealing that a fast food company, "Hot an' Fast," purchased beef raised on deforested rainforest land. Destroying rainforests in order to raise cheap beef threatens the delicate environmental balance of the earth. Your community has a "Hot an' Fast" restaurant. People enjoy eating there because the restaurant manager donates money and advertisement to the local high school's football team. Despite this, your grassroots group believes in the Defenders of Animals' cause. What will you do?

Options

1. Write a letter of protest to the national headquarters of "Hot an' Fast."

2. Educate people to choose alternative foods, like hot fish sandwiches, and skip the beef.

3. Organize a protest in front of the restaurant and heighten the public's awareness of rainforest destruction.

4. Other _____

_____

Trash Heap, a national watchdog environmental group, reported in your local newspaper that the company that is managing your community's landfill has been illegally burying hazardous waste. Trash Heap contends that the company engages in this illegal practice for enormous profits. The company counters that Trash Heap is a group of radicals out to stir up trouble. The company issued a statement that it would close the landfill if Trash Heap continued to stick its nose in the company's business. Shutting down the landfill would be costly to your community. Nevertheless, your grassroots group wants action! What will you do?

Options

1. Join forces with the Trash Heap group and keep media attention on the landfill company.

2. Circulate a petition requesting that state officials investigate whether hazardous waste is being buried in the landfill.

3. Donate money to support the cause of Trash Heap.

4. Other _____

_____

Now that you have become involved in environmental activism, think about the choices you have made. Is it easy or difficult to make choices? If you completed this strategy in a group, did you feel pressure to change any of your opinions and options? What are you learning about your ecological values? Refer to your Values Journal and make a few notations.

Risky Stuff

Risky Stuff gets at the heart of value clarification and decisions—we take *risks* when we follow our real values. Some risks mean sticking our necks out. Others may mean taking an unpopular stand on a particular issue. We might risk criticism or even rejection from others. When we take a risk, we're not always certain what will happen. We can't predict how others will react to our public opinions and actions.

Risky Stuff describes five risk-taking situations that call for your opinion and action. You need to decide what you will do and weigh possible risks. You will have to decide what risks you will face if you choose certain actions.

Each situation describes an event that involves you and a group, like a group of friends or a committee. If you work on this strategy in a class or club, other members can be selected to be part of the group or committee. Undoubtedly they will not remain passive or quiet in these strategies! They will want to know the risks you are about to take.

One

You are with friends at a shopping mall. Everyone is having fun browsing in the stores and watching the crowd of shoppers. One of your friends sees a huge coat sale at a fur store and wants to investigate the savings. Your friends know that you love animals, so they dare you to go into the store. What will you do?

Possible risks: _____

_____

Your response: _____

_____

Two   You have pledged to reduce red meat in your diet. You have
                 not become a vegetarian but you are thinking about the
                 possibility. You have been invited to spend a week at your
                 relative's summer cottage. You know they enjoy cooking all
                 meals on their grill, especially steaks and hamburgers. What
                 will you do?

Possible risks: _____

_____

Your response: _____

_____

Three   You are on the Homecoming Dance Planning Committee.
                 Your job is to order one thousand drinking cups and small
                 plates for snacks and finger food. The clean-up committee
                 is pressuring you to order cheap, disposable plastic cups
                 and plates. They argue that this will help reduce the costs
                 for the dance as well as make cleaning up an easy job. You
                 object to more plastic being dumped in landfills. What will
                 you do?

Possible risks: _____

_____

Your response: _____

_____

Four   You and three other friends are planning an all-day sight-seeing trip. Everyone agrees that the trip should be in the North Woods and include a stop at a canoe rental site. One friend has a car and wants to travel as far as possible in one day. You would prefer a bike trip which could still include canoeing. You argue that saving fuel is part of a meaningful trip to the North Woods. Your friends counter that everyone else drives cars, so there is little reason to try to conserve fuel. How will you work this out with your friends?

Possible risks: _____

_____

Your response: _____

_____

Five   You are on the student council. You are concerned that the school's maintenance department uses harmful pesticides on the grounds. You have tried to raise this issue before the council. No one wants to listen. Most members think you're just a "nature nut." One member secretly confides that your concern might be valid but does not want to support you publicly. The member urges you to write a letter to the editor of the school newspaper. What will you do?

Possible risks: _____

_____

Your response: _____

_____

What is it like to take risks? How does it feel to stand up for
your beliefs? How do your friends react to your opinions?
What are you learning about social needs, like approval and
acceptance, and following your values?

You're the President

Do you believe that the president of the United States has
power to help save the environment? Certainly we can all
agree that the president has enormous executive powers.
And former presidents like Theodore Roosevelt, Richard
Nixon, and Jimmy Carter, used their executive authority to
enact legislation to preserve land and help clean the air and
water. But just how much power does a president wield in
any given situation? In our country, politicians are influenced by high-powered lobbying or special interest groups.
Lobbying is an attempt to influence the decisions of government officials.

In Washington, lawmakers, presidential advisors, and
cabinet officials are surrounded by outside lobbyists. Lobbyists try to persuade legislators to vote in a particular way. A
lobbyist may be a member of a group interested in a particular law or policy.

Environmental groups like Defenders of Wildlife, Sierra Club, and the National Wildlife Federation lobby for bills
that will conserve energy, help clean the air and water, and
protect fragile environments. There are powerful business
and industrial groups that lobby for their economic interests. Sometimes environmental groups and business lobbyists agree on certain policies. At other times they strongly
disagree. For example, the National Wildlife Federation and
other conservation groups have lobbied to protect land and
endangered wildlife. On the other hand, lumber companies

have pressured lawmakers to modify laws that protect endangered species so that more forests can be cleared.

The president of the United States is confronted with many large-scale problems. The president has to consult with his advisors and other interested parties. But he is also going to be influenced by lobbying groups.

In the strategy *You're the President* you will be president of the United States. Divide your friends or other group participants into two lobbying groups. One group represents environmentalists. The other group represents organizations who want bills passed for economic gain, regardless of the effect on the earth.

As president, not only must you direct policies that will keep our country strong but your decisions have long-range *consequences*. If you execute policies that reduce oil consumption and conserve energy, oil company lobbyists might protest that this will drastically reduce industry profits and in turn this will hurt the U.S. economy. So what is the president to do? What would you do?

Spotted Owl Protection

When you campaigned for the presidency, you promised to pass tougher laws that would protect endangered wildlife. Now that you are president, your advisors have urged you to soften your position. The country's economy suddenly hits a slump. Lobbyists from the American Log Haulers Association (ALHA) are pressing you to weaken the endangered wildlife laws as well as policies that protect forests. Yet if the forests are destroyed, the endangered spotted owl will become extinct. Logging officials believe that is the price of progress and saving jobs. Lobbyists representing Save the Animals are leading a drive to strengthen wildlife laws. A massive letter-writing campaign has been launched urging you to "Give a Hoot." As president, will you pass strong or weak wildlife protection laws?

What are the possible *consequences* of your decision?

_____

_____

What is the best thing that can happen as a result of your decision?

_____

_____

What is the worst thing that can happen as a result of your decision?

_____

_____

Ban Pesticides

Pesticides manufactured by Pesty Pest Eliminators Corporation (PPEC) have been banned in the United States. It is reported that the chemicals in the bug killing products are harmful to human health. Lobbyists representing Pesty Pest Eliminators Corporation are working to change laws that prohibit selling and shipping their product to foreign countries. Lobbying groups from Americans for Sane Use of Chemicals and Mothers Against Harmful Pesticides argue that the pesticides should not be exported, especially to poor third world countries. Yet government officials in those foreign countries do not care if they purchase chemicals which have been banned in the U.S. They realize that the pesticides are very useful in their agricultural interests. They have sent ambassadors to support the lobbyists from Pesty Pest Eliminators Corporation. As president, which group will you listen to? Will you change the laws that ban shipment of harmful chemicals? Do you have a responsibility to maintain friendly relationships with other countries? What will you do?

What are the possible *consequences* of your decision?

_____

_____

Being in a position of power is different from exercising power. Having an impressive title is not enough nor is it the only qualification to influence change in our society. *How* you use your powers—the decisions you make and the consequences of your decisions—is more significant. Make notations in your Values Journal about the importance of studying consequences when making value choices.

The Green Thumb Award

You have been hired as the director of the Parks and Recreation Department of your city, Mainstreet, U.S.A. You have been instructed to select a team of Parks and Recreation Department employees to brainstorm ideas to help promote a clean, green image for Mainstreet, U.S.A. The city council believes that if the city had high standards for a "green" or ecology-minded community, this would attract outside businesses to relocate in the area. If this project is successful, the President's Council on Greener Communities could award Mainstreet, U.S.A. the national Green Thumb Award. This would give much publicity to the city. Such recognition would also boost your career!

You call your team together for a brainstorming meeting to collect ideas for the project. You instruct the team that *brainstorming is a technique to come up with as many ideas as possible to a series of questions.* Members are allowed to say whatever comes to mind, no matter how silly or outrageous the idea. Brainstorming encourages freedom to express one's thoughts and to be as creative as possible. After all ideas are listed on a piece of paper, then the group reviews them and begins to select ideas they want to work on.

The *Green Thumb Award* can be used at home or at school. Family members, friends, and classmates will find this exercise challenging and stimulating. Gather at least 3-5 individuals (or more) to serve as the team.

FIRST, encourage the team to brainstorm a technique called "Reverse Imaging." In reverse imaging the team comes up with as many ideas about how to get the *reverse* of what they want to accomplish. If the goal is to come up with ideas to create a healthy, clean Mainstreet, U.S.A. environment, *what is the reverse of this?* How many ideas can the team come up with to make Mainstreet, U.S.A. a dirty, polluted place in which to live? How many ideas can the group come up with that show how we could pollute the environment, harm the wildlife, and make the air unbreathable? What would make Mainstreet, U.S.A. a rotten place to live in? Take five minutes to list as many ideas as possible. Use other sheets of paper if necessary.

1. Throw garbage in streets.

2. _____

3. _____

4. _____

5. _____

6. _____

7. _____

8. _____

9. _____

10. _____

11. _____

12. _____

13. _____   17. _____

14. _____   18. _____

15. _____   19. _____

16. _____   20. _____

SECOND, encourage the team to come up with as many ideas as possible that will help promote an ecology-minded image for Mainstreet, U.S.A. Take ten minutes to complete this part. Remember that this is a time to dream and envision a healthy place in which to live, have fun, go to school, and work, a place to be proud of.

Beautification Envision a city where humans, animals, flowers, rivers, trees, and birds can exist together. Brainstorm ideas about how to make Mainstreet, U.S.A. clean and beautiful. Would you have a recycling program? Would people have a campaign to plant flowers and trees? Ban vehicles that pollute the air? Tear down abandoned buildings? Never allow buildings to become abandoned?

1. _____   8. _____

2. _____   9. _____

3. _____   10. _____

4. _____   11. _____

5. _____   12. _____

6. _____   13. _____

7. _____   14. _____

15. _____   18. _____

16. _____   19. _____

17. _____   20. _____

Recreation   How will people have fun without mistreating the environ-
                      ment? What kind of play equipment would you install in
                      parks and at schools? Would you build bike paths and set
                      aside special places for exercise, walking, and jogging?
                      Would you pass laws that protect wildlife?

1. _____   11. _____

2. _____   12. _____

3. _____   13. _____

4. _____   14. _____

5. _____   15. _____

6. _____   16. _____

7. _____   17. _____

8. _____   18. _____

9. _____   19. _____

10. _____   20. _____

Citizen   How can citizens of all ages take pride in Mainstreet,
Participation   U.S.A.? How can people help keep the environment clean
                      and beautiful? Will they be able to help plant trees? Clean
                      rivers? Build playground equipment?

1. _____   11. _____

2. _____   12. _____

3. _____   13. _____

4. _____   14. _____

5. _____   15. _____

6. _____   16. _____

7. _____   17. _____

8. _____   18. _____

9. _____   19. _____

10. _____   20. _____

THIRD, STOP the exercise and take several minutes to review all of the positive ideas.

As director, it is your responsibility to draw up a plan to promote a green image. Examine the ideas that your team has suggested. *Choose* three of the most creative ideas listed in each category: beautification, recreation, and citizen participation. Circle your choices.

Examine your final choices.

What kind of image will your city take pride in? How will Mainstreet, U.S.A. be viewed by outside businesses, tourists, and the President's Council on Greener Communities? Will you receive the Green Thumb Award?

_____

_____

_____

_____

Refer to your Values Journal and make a few notations. What could you do to make your home or yard receive a "Green Thumb Award"? Could your school receive a "Green Thumb Award"? Review your notations on aesthetic nature values and recreational values. Did this exercise reveal your nature-oriented values?

Part Three
Eco-Values in Action

"Unless you try to do something beyond
what you have already mastered,
you will never grow."

— *Ronald E. Osborn*

Eco-Role Models

When we grasp the severity of our environmental crisis, the problems may seem overwhelming. One might wonder if a person can truly help to effect positive change.

Well there is a lot that each of us can do to contribute to positive ecology. We can do positive things to help save the earth. By discovering and following one's eco-values, change can occur in one's family, neighborhood, church, and community and even in the global community.

Let's face it, we are an impatient culture. We expect a quick fix to complex ecological problems. This just won't happen. Expecting easy answers only adds to a sense of hopelessness.

Today, more than ever, we need to see that individuals can make a difference. How can we do this? One way is to study the lives and values of individuals who influenced positive ecology in our western culture. There are six individuals who have had a profound impact on our knowledge of the earth and earth-sensitive values. These six include: St. Francis of Assisi, Henry David Thoreau, John Muir, Albert Schweitzer, Aldo Leopold, and Rachel Carson. While there are many other ecologists who have made fine contributions, these six deserve special attention and merit. They sought an intimate relationship with the divine creator and were willing to do his will in the kingdom on earth. They took personal risk to follow their spiritual faith and eco-values. Each acted with deep conviction. They are inspirational role models.

We need to examine the lives of people who have lived, breathed, and experienced their ecological values. It is especially important to see how people have grappled with their values and how this struggle has actually enriched their lives and ours. In this way we are able to see what it means to take responsibility for one's earth-sensitive values and how this can make a positive difference.

SCRIPTURE-SPEAK

"As each has received a gift, employ it for one another" (1 Pet 4:10).

St. Francis of Assisi

"Praised be you, my Lord, with all your creatures."

If anyone was an unlikely candidate for ecology or sainthood, it was St. Francis. As a youth he enjoyed a wealthy and carefree lifestyle. How Francis came to be devoted to Christ, poverty, charity, and love of nature is an extraordinary story.

Francis was born in the town of Assisi set in the hills of Umbria in Italy in 1181. His father, Peter Bernardone, was a merchant and had a prosperous trade with France. His mother, Pica, was a gentle woman and from good circumstances. The Bernardones were well-to-do and Francis was destined to live a comfortable life.

Historians have found it difficult to examine St. Francis' life and contribution to spiritual ecology. Much of his life is buried in myth and events have been poorly recorded. For example, Francis allegedly pacified a hungry wolf by reminding the man-eating predator of his membership in the Christian fellowship. As we are about to see, Francis did offer a spiritual vision of a community where all living things co-exist. This is a profound insight into enlightened ideas about ecology, considering the period when Francis lived.

In his youth Francis was devoted to the ideals of romantic chivalry. He had plenty of money and spent it lavishly. He was uninterested in his father's business and in formal learning. Francis was rather self-centered and bent on enjoying himself. Despite his free-wheeling lifestyle, he never refused to give alms to any poor fellow who asked it of him for the love of the heavenly Father.

Touched by Compassion

When Francis was about twenty, strife broke out between the cities of Assisi and Perugia, and Francis was carted off a prisoner by the Perugians. After about a year he was released, only to be struck down by a long and dangerous sickness. Upon his recovery Francis was determined to join the forces of Walter de Brienne, who was fighting in southern Italy. His dreams of romantic chivalry were about to be fulfilled. Francis bought himself expensive equipment and set out to meet up with de Brienne's forces. Along the way he met a gentleman reduced to poverty and very ill-clad. He was deeply touched with compassion and, without hesitation, changed clothes with the man. Unwittingly Francis did more than exchange garments. The change of clothes was the first visible step in a series of behaviors which resulted in Francis radically changing his values and attitudes toward the world around him.

The Journey Begins

Francis' journey took an ironic twist. He never did reach the battlefront. At Spoleto he was taken ill again, and as he lay recuperating, a heavenly voice seemed to tell him to turn back, to serve God rather than man. Francis obeyed, yet he did not know the full meaning of the message. At first he returned to his old lifestyle, but something was missing. He found himself being more restrained and his carefree behavior seemed less enjoyable. Something inside Francis stirred him to prayer and he had a desire to sell his goods. He was uncertain of the course that his life was about to embark on, but he sensed that he was being converted to Christ's gospels. Strong inspirations were overcoming Francis as he turned his life over to prayer and reading the gospels.

Riding one day through the plain of Assisi, he came upon a leper whose sores were so loathsome that at the sight of them he was struck with horror. Ordinarily Francis would have acknowledged such a disfigured man with a nod or an alms, but he would have moved on quickly. On this day he dismounted, and as the leper stretched out his hand to receive an alms, Francis, as he bestowed it, kissed the man. He was overwhelmed with compassion and experienced a deep sense of humility. The encounter caused a remarkable change in Francis. Henceforward he often visited the hospitals and served the sick and gave freely to the poor. He sometimes gave the needy his clothes and money. He followed the gospel command, "Blest are the lowly; they shall inherit the land" (Mt 5:5).

Francis' changed behavior did not go unnoticed by the citizens of Assisi. Some thought he had gone mad. His change of heart and values put him at odds with his father. When Francis sold a horseload of cloth out of his father's warehouse in order to help pay for repairs of a local church, the father became enraged. This led to a confrontation in which Peter demanded that his son either come to his senses and stop such nonsense or renounce all his share in the family inheritance. Francis had no objection to being disinherited; he aimed to serve Christ. The father distanced himself from his son, although he felt profound sorrow.

Francis went in search of some convenient shelter. He sought out a monastery and labored as an unknown poor man. In return for his work, Francis accepted alms.

Francis traveled the countryside and visited the sick and needy. He dressed simply and walked with a staff in hand. He lived the gospel calling, "You are the salt of the earth" (Mt 5:13). His good deeds were noticed.

A New Way of Life

Many began to admire Francis, and some desired to be his companion and follow his ways. The first of these was Bernard da Quintavalle, a rich tradesman of Assisi. He watched the career of Francis with curiosity and respect. He invited Francis to stay in his home for a while. Bernard was struck by Francis' sincerity and humility. Together they read the scriptures, and Bernard asked Francis to make him a disciple. Bernard sold all of his goods and divided his money among the poor. Two other men asked Francis if they could join his new lifestyle dedicated to charity and works of mercy. One was the famous Brother Giles, an individual of profound simplicity and spiritual wisdom. When his followers had increased to about a dozen, Francis drew up a short informed rule and took it to Rome in 1210 for the pope's approval. His order was founded on the principles of poverty and charity and the teachings of Christ. An interesting point is that Francis would not own property for his new community of disciples. He shied away from any notion of dominion over the land. He was more interested in his order working the land and giving goods to the needy than in acquiring property for the sake of ownership. The seeds of ecology, community, and equality were seen early in the formation of Francis' order.

Out of humility Francis gave to his order the name of Friars Minor and the brothers labored to raise money for alms for the poor. For their daily bread the brothers worked in the fields for neighboring farmers. When work

was lacking, they begged door to door and asked to perform some service. They gave their offerings to lepers and
other sufferers. Francis referred to his followers as "my
brother Christians" and encouraged them to labor for
goods which were immediately turned over to the less for-
tunate and sick. He saw those who suffered as an extension
of his community.

Enlightened Ideas About the Earth

Francis was struck by the words of Christ. "Look at the birds
in the sky. They do not sow or reap, they gather nothing
into barns; yet your heavenly Father feeds them" (Mt 6:26).
In his spiritual maturity, Francis regarded all life-forms as
"brothers" and "sisters" in the community of God. He frequently used the term "mother" to characterize the earth.
He had a new or enlightened way of seeing things. His concept of enlightened and spiritual ecology is seen in the following prayer of gratitude.

> Most High, all powerful, good Lord,
> to you all praise, glory and honor
> and all blessing;
> to you alone, Most High, they belong
> and no man is worthy of naming you.
>
> Praised be you, my Lord,
> With all your creatures,
> especially, my Lord, Brother Sun,
> who brings day, and by whom you enlighten us;
> he is beautiful, he shines with great splendor;
> of you, Most High, he is the symbol.
>
> Praised to you, my Lord,
> for Sister Moon and the Stars;
> in the heavens you formed them,
> clear, precious and beautiful.

Praised be you, my Lord, for Brother Wind
and for the air and for the clouds,
for the azure calm and for all climes
by which you give life to your creatures.

Praised be you, my Lord, for Sister Water,
who is very useful and humble,
precious and chaste.

Praised be you, my Lord, for Brother Fire,
by which you enlighten the night:
he is beautiful and joyous,
indomitable and strong.

Praised be you, my Lord,
for Sister our Mother the Earth
who nourishes us and bears us,
and produces all kinds of fruits,
with the speckled flowers and the herbs.

For Francis, all creatures and natural processes had a direct relationship with the divine creator.

The Earth as Sacred

Francis' beliefs and teachings about ecology were radical and completely unprecedented in Christian history. Had his philosophy been carefully examined by church authorities, Francis might have been condemned as a heretic. Yet his teachings on his love of God and concern for the poor made him popular. This overshadowed his beliefs about nature and how the earth was part of his community. *Breaking from the thinking of the day, Francis believed that all of nature had sacred value and this value was not to be defined solely by human interests.*

Francis died on October 3, 1226 after a long illness claimed his health and life. He was about forty-five years old. As was typical of his humility, he asked to be buried in a criminals' cemetery. The religious order he founded continued to be inspired by his love of God, works of charity, and giving to the poor. It would be decades later that theologians would once again turn to his thoughts and beliefs about nature.

In the 1960s, theologians began to challenge the age-old belief that mankind had a right to conquest and rule over nature. They searched for guidance in order to develop a Christian ethical philosophy that embraced a unity with nature. They turned to the writings of St. Francis and his insights into the ecological community. They appreciated how, in beautiful simplicity, St. Francis separated birds, rocks, wolves, and rivers from the category of "things" by introducing them with humans in a single spiritual fellowship. To Francis, all life and matter was in God's community. His vision would later be expanded by Pierre Teilhard de Chardin, a priest and scientist in the 1950s. Chardin concluded from his scientific works that not only would nature be holy but the universe or cosmos would be sacred. By the 1960s, theologians and scientists had included atoms and cosmic particles into the vast Christian membership and moral ethics. Undoubtedly St. Francis would have smiled at such wisdom!

Patron Saint of Ecology

In 1960 the University of Michigan zoologist, Marston Bates, declared that for Christians who valued nature, St. Francis of Assisi was their rightful patron. In 1967 historian Lynn White called St. Francis "a patron saint for ecologists." White believed that St. Francis challenged Christian anthropocentrism and the dualism that separated humanity from nature. After reviewing the writings and teachings of St. Francis, White pointed out that the saint's ecological beliefs held no hierarchies, no chain of beings, and no dualism which put man at odds with the earth. White marveled at how, in simple song and prayer, ants, worms, and birds were just as much a part of the saint's community of worshipers as the higher primates. Anticipating Albert Schweitzer by seven centuries, St. Francis commonly removed worms and little creatures from foot paths so they would be spared being crushed. Historian White wrote several articles advocating that St. Francis be the saint of ecology. In 1980 the Vatican acted on these recommendations and officially named Francis the patron saint of ecologists.

St. Francis has appealed to Catholics and Protestants alike. His extraordinary simplicity has captured imaginations throughout history.

Doing God's Will

In terms of ecological value development, St. Francis shows what it means to be devoted to doing God's will on earth. He did not take lightly the command to love God, love one's neighbor, even one's enemies, and to respect nature. In the end he gave us a vision of community where all living species are regarded as equals in the eyes of the divine creator.

One last interesting point that I feel needs to be discussed is how St. Francis attracted others to his beliefs. St. Francis simply *lived* his Christian values and people recognized his sincerity. There is an old saying that "action speaks louder than words." St. Francis exercised this and, in turn, other people wanted to follow his ways. For each of us we can see how this example applies in our own lives, relationships with others, and stewardship with the earth.

Henry David Thoreau

"We need the tonic of wildness."

If each of us would touch the life of another species, the quality of life on this planet would be greatly enhanced. Henry David Thoreau's eco-values reached all life-forms. He battled for the rights of slaves and extended his concern to ecology. His ideas were ridiculed but he stood fast by his values. His story is one of courage.

Henry David Thoreau was born in Concord, Massachusetts, on July 12, 1817. Unlike most leading writers and intellectuals of his time, Thoreau came from a family that was neither wealthy nor distinguished. Henry's father made pencils in a small shop. His mother took in boarders.

Thoreau graduated from Harvard College at the age of twenty. He soon met the writer Ralph Waldo Emerson, who greatly encouraged him to write, offered him constructive criticism, and later employed him as a handyman and gardener. Emerson also introduced Thoreau to the philosophy of life that combined science and reason with mysticism. Emerson insisted that man should learn as much as possible through observation, science, and reason. He also emphasized a life of simplicity, self-reliance and individuality. Emerson's influence emerged in many of Thoreau's journals.

Value of Individual Freedom

Thoreau strongly believed that each citizen must be free to act according to one's own idea of right and wrong, without government interference. The writer summarized his idea of the role of government in "Civil Disobedience" (1849). He observed that there will never be a truly free and enlightened state until the state recognizes the power of the individual and the individual's contribution to the state. The essay strongly influenced Leo Tolstoy, Mahatma Gandhi, and Martin Luther King. For his part, Thoreau called for an end to black slavery. He attacked it in the essay "Slavery in Massachusetts" (1854), and openly defended abolitionist John Brown's raid at Harpers Ferry.

What really disturbed Thoreau was his fellow man's exploitation of the earth's resources. He was displeased that people seemed to be indifferent about his plea for a simpler lifestyle.

Displeasure with Materialism

Thoreau deliberately chose July 4, 1845 for his departure to Walden Pond near Concord, Massachusetts. He wanted to make a statement! The naturalist-philosopher saw little reason to celebrate the nation's sixty-ninth birthday. Americans seemed to be obsessed with what Emerson called "things" or material possessions. What really unnerved Thoreau was a trip to a local shop to purchase a blank notebook in which to record his thoughts. The writer was an avid journal keeper. To his horror, Thoreau could only find ledgers that were ruled for dollars and cents. It struck him that his countrymen seemed to be governed by values of self-interest. He stood outside the shop, gazed about, and sadly shook his head. The new world was only an object, an expansive resource, and Americans were exploiting it with an unquenchable hunger. Thoreau seriously questioned the inexhaustibility of America's forests and soil. He had already witnessed the rapid recession of the New England woodlands.

Walden

Walden Pond inspired Thoreau's most famous book, *Walden* (1854). He lived alone near the pond for almost two years. *Walden* vividly records Thoreau's observations of nature there, and tells how he built his one-room cabin, paid his bills, raised a vegetable garden, and spent his time. It also tells about his visitors and reports what he read, reflected on, and thought. On a deeper level, *Walden* is a celebration of a human being living in harmony with nature.

Thoreau insisted that his trip to Walden Pond was an experiment in simple living, not a passive withdrawal from society. He appealed to his fellow Americans to economize, to simplify their lifestyles, and to respect nature. Many of his ideas and a plea to live in harmony with the earth fell on seemingly deaf ears.

Thoreau was influenced by the naturalists, botanists, and religious writers of that era. The idea that nature consisted of different parts (rocks, soil, flowers, and wildlife) fitting together was taking shape in the minds of scientific and religious circles. In 1793 the Reverend Nicholas Collin addressed the American Philosophical Society with a loud plea to support the protection of little-known birds on the verge of extinction. Collins advised that naturalists should discover what part they played in the study of nature. Thoreau was impressed with the enlightened thinkers who saw the study of nature fitting into the expanded concept of a community fellowship where its membership had a right to protection.

The Earth as Community

Thoreau always enjoyed daily walks in the New England countryside. He took notice of the varieties of vegetation, trees, and wildlife. He believed that the earth was a living body, not a dead mass. He also observed how organisms related to each other. *This led him to conclude that nature and its creatures made up a society.* He wrote in his journals that animals were not beasts but "fellows" or "neighbors" and members of his society. He came to believe that forests were not a wilderness to be tamed by an axe but a "civilization" of wildlife, plants, and organisms. Such ideas about the economy of nature were radical for that period of history.

You might be struck by the similar ideas of St. Francis of Assisi and Henry David Thoreau. Both believed that animals, plants, and other species as well as the human species lived together in a community of God. Both proposed in their writings an enlightened and broad perspective of community.

A New Ethics

Thoreau did not write about the rights of nature per se, but he did imply that humanity's interaction with the earth must be guided by ethics. Morality must take a wide view of the universe. He observed that just as there are people who are prosecuted for abusing children, others deserve to be prosecuted for maltreating nature. He was horrified by Concord farmers who stripped the land of trees and underbrush, thus opening the ecosystems to soil erosion.

To say that Thoreau was a visionary of twentieth century environmental ethics would be an understatement. His association of abused people with abused nature placed him squarely in the line of environmental activists who combine fighting for the rights of the oppressed with the rights of nature. His ideals would influence present day activists like Gary Snyder, Peter Singer, and David Brower.

Thoreau's ecological philosophy was not welcomed by an emerging nation that believed it was blessed with unlimited resources. Quite possibly only a handful of Americans even read Thoreau's essays on nature. Some who did ridiculed and eventually ignored him.

We all have a basic need to be loved and accepted by others. Sometimes this very human need can be in conflict with our values to stand up for what is right. There may be times when we take a stand on environmental pollution or the neglect of the earth, and this may prove to be unpopular with others. Thoreau showed us how to act on eco-values with deep conviction, even in the face of criticism.

John Muir

"Everything is hitched to everything else."

Have you ever wondered how a peacemaker and an ecologist have similar eco-values? The fascinating story of John Muir tells how this is so.

Muir's life began on April 21, 1838, when he was born in Dunbar, a tiny Scottish seaport near Edinburgh. John had two older sisters and a younger brother. The Muirs resided in a big stone house, part of which was the family store. John's father sold supplies to farmers and had a dream that someday he would own a farm in the United States.

As a youngster, John explored the rocky shores of the North Sea with his brother David. The two boys collected pocketfuls of shells and seaweed. They observed eels and crabs that had been trapped among the rocks at low tide.

New Life Skills

As the boys grew in strength, they played in the ruins of Dunbar Castle, high above the town. The castle had been built a thousand years before to defend Scotland from its enemies. John and David had avid and playful imaginations, and they relived the drama of the castle's honor.

John showed exceptional skills at climbing the castle walls. Twenty years later he used these skills to climb mountains and trekked across glaciers in Alaska. His physical abilities allowed him to explore American wilderness that proved too dangerous for amateur hikers and climbers.

When John was eleven years old, his father had saved sufficient funds to move to America and purchase some farm land on the shores of a lake in Wisconsin. The land was surrounded by wilderness and was a dense habitat for fox, raccoons, deer, bear, large turtles, and a variety of songbirds. John's lively imagination and interest in natural things was phenomenal. He had a strong urge to explore the woodlands and meadows and quietly observe the wildlife. He came to believe that the land belongs to animals as much as it does to people. This was a belief he would carry into his national park campaign. The values of humans and animals co-existing were emerging in his thoughts and observations.

Hardship and Responsibility

During his adolescence, John labored on the farm sixteen hours a day. In the spring of each year he worked hard, plowing, planting, and hoeing. During the winter John was responsible for caring for the livestock and chopping and hauling wood for the fireplace. When he wasn't working, his father insisted that he read the Bible. His father shunned formal education and reading books. He was convinced that the Bible was the only book human beings needed. This eventually led to a riff between the father and his son.

Despite his father's loud protest and threats, Muir enrolled in the University of Wisconsin. He was committed to getting an education and supported himself by doing odd jobs. Muir became especially engrossed in botany and geology. He was fascinated by the study of glaciers and how the once vast ice fields had shaped the earth. John often took day-long trips into wild areas to study plants and rock formations. He showed a keen eye for sizing up and understanding a particular habitat with its relationship of rocks, soil, vegetation, and animals.

"Earth Planet — Universe"

Upon graduation from the university, Muir was determined to live in the wilderness and study nature. He traveled about, continuing to support himself with odd jobs and manual labor. On foot he traveled to Indiana and then to Kentucky. As he hiked through woodlands he gathered plants and drew sketches of them in his notebook. By this time John and his father were no longer on speaking terms. John could not return to the farm unless he abandoned his seemingly foolish notion to study nature. He was expected to settle down to farm work. Under no other terms would he be welcome. Hence, John left home and stated to a friend that his new address was "Earth Planet—Universe."

At this juncture in his career the Civil War was raging. President Abraham Lincoln requested 500,000 more men to defend the Union on March 10, 1864. Muir was twenty-six years old and single. He felt certain that he would be called. John was a peacemaker who believed in non-violence. He was devoted to the Bible and the Christian command to love one's enemies. He was sensitive to the foibles of humanity and refused to divide people into "good" and "bad" categories. He also cared greatly for nature. So Muir left Wisconsin and vanished into the Canadian wilderness north of Lake Huron. The experience would prove to have a lasting impact on his earth-sensitive values.

Muir followed a rugged trail into a wet and darkening swamp where he came upon a cluster of rare white orchids. He sat down beside them and was suddenly overwhelmed with joy. Reflecting later on the experience, Muir realized that his spontaneous emotion sprang from the fact that the "goodness" of the rare orchids did not have the slightest relevance to his presence. Nature simply exists for itself and the divine creator. Everything has unique value, and this worth does not depend on human judgment.

"A Rightful Place"

Being alone in the wilderness allowed Muir time to reflect on his relationship with God. He was struck with the perfect beauty of virgin forests. He concluded that God permeated the earth. He further reasoned that human beings were members of a community that included rocks, soil, wildlife, plants (like the orchids), reptiles, birds, and even skunks. *Everything had a rightful and sacred place on earth.*

Muir thought about passages from the Bible and his refusal to see people as good or bad. Once again, these were human judgments and categories. Observing the Canadian woodlands and swamps, Muir reasoned that nature could not be divided up into good-bad categories, defined by human interests. Later, he was asked the question, "What good are rattlesnakes for?" He replied that they were good for themselves. Snakes were beautiful in the eyes of the divine creator. To say that snakes were either good *or* bad reflected man's ignorance of other species and also showed deep-seated prejudices. Following identical thoughts of St. Francis of Assisi, Muir was convinced that all creatures were loved by God. He developed a philosophy of environmental ethics.

After the Civil War, Muir hiked through Tennessee and North Carolina. He encountered many black people who had been slaves and was struck by how they had attained freedom, yet many were wandering aimlessly, and he felt compassion for them. Once when he was hungry a black family gave him supper. Although they were dirt-poor, they freely shared their cornbread with the Yankee stranger. He recorded this experience in his journal. Muir often thought about the simple generosity and kindness of that family when he confronted humanity's ignorance, prejudice and brutality.

National Parks

Muir became a national hero for defining the values of a vanishing wilderness and championing the national park idea. He was convinced that the only way to save the vast forests was to publicly proclaim their useful value. He knew that lawmakers were not likely to support the idea that rattlesnakes were loved by their creator. Nor would they listen to how redwood trees had natural rights. He did not wish to invite ridicule from Congress, nor from the public. He knew that people would be swayed by the belief that the wilderness should be saved for future generations to enjoy and that national parks were lovely places for hiking, camping, and aesthetic values and enjoyment. Muir confined his thoughts about environmental ethics to his private journals and to himself. He knew that people would not understand his ideas about spiritual ecological values.

The establishment of Yosemite National Park in 1890 was Muir's greatest political achievement, although he had other important achievements. A significant event occurred in our country's history and conservation movement. John Muir met President Theodore Roosevelt (1858-1919). Both men had an interest in preserving nature but for different reasons. Muir had a broad, spiritual view. Roosevelt saw nature from utilitarian values or what was most useful to society. Roosevelt had been a former cattle rancher before becoming our twenty-sixth president. He understood the utilitarian value of setting aside land for human interests like hunting, recreation, and raising cattle. Muir influenced Roosevelt to set aside millions of acres of land for national parks and conservation interests.

Protecting National Parks

Muir knew that national parks would need special protection. A group of Californians organized around Muir for the purpose of defending the new parks. They called themselves the Sierra Club. In 1908 the Sierra Club began an unsuccessful campaign to prevent San Francisco from taking a major portion of Yosemite National Park, the Hetch Hetchy Valley, and developing it into a municipal water and hydropower facility.

The defeat of the Hetch Hetchy Valley campaign took a terrible toll on Muir's health. Protecting the wilderness had become his holy war. When the San Francisco dam project was officially unveiled, Muir lashed out at the supporting politicians and newspapers. To Muir, nature's wilderness was a cathedral. He called his opponents "temple destroyers" who were flirting with "Satan and Company." His preservation crusade took on a moral intensity, but in the end the Sierra Club lost its fight to save the valley. The defeat almost broke his heart. Soon afterward, in 1914, he died. The vast and beautiful Hetch Hetchy Valley was buried forever under tons of water.

Some readers might conclude that environmentalism is rather futile—look at what ultimately happened to John Muir and the Hetch Hetchy Valley. Yet I don't believe in pessimism. Human events need to be seen realistically. Quite simply, we win some environmental battles and lose others. Even in the losses, however, there are positive gains. Not everyone in Muir's day agreed with flooding the valley. The publicity generated public sentiment. Some folks were outraged. Member-

ship in the Sierra Club increased, and today the club continues to preserve national parks, canyons, and seashores as well
as fight for clean air and water legislation. Hence, Muir did
not die in vain. He was committed to Christian love and environmental ethics. He showed us the political maneuvering
necessary to win congressional support. Muir helped to
launch the Sierra Club and the value of activism and networking. An individual cannot fight alone for the rights of nature,
or to right a wrong. Joining with other groups and people
who want to preserve the earth increases our chances to win
environmental battles. John Muir will be remembered for
these outstanding contributions.

Albert Schweitzer

"We need boundless ethics which will include the animals also."

One interesting thing about eco-value development is that a person is not always certain where their journey into ecology and related spirituality will lead. When Albert Schweitzer was enjoying an international reputation as an organist, he did not dream that one day he would be concerned about the lowly creatures of the earth.

In order to appreciate Albert Schweitzer the man, the humanitarian, and the ecological philosopher, we need to examine events that were occurring in the United States and Europe. By 1900 there was a serious attempt by writers, ecological philosophers, and humanitarians to exchange ideas across the ocean. Schweitzer was well educated and had a large appetite for books. He was open to new ideas, beliefs, and values, especially regarding animal protection.

International Fame

Schweitzer was born on January 14, 1875, at Kayserberg, Alsace, and was educated in both France and Germany. At the age of twenty-one Albert decided to spend his next nine years concentrating on music, science, and preaching God's word, and then to devote the rest of his life to serving humanity, especially the sick and lame, directly. Before he was thirty years old, he had won an international reputation as a writer on theology, as an organist, and as an interpreter of the works of Johann Sebastian Bach. Schweitzer could entertain kings and queens and converse with the wealthy and powerful elite of society as well as discuss passages of the Bible with noted theologians.

In 1902 Schweitzer became principal of St. Thomas Theological College at the University of Strasbourg. It was at this point in his career that Schweitzer had a profound conversion experience that changed the meaning of his life. Despite his notoriety he felt that something was missing in his life. He prayed and listened to God's voice. He was inspired to become a medical missionary, and he studied medicine from 1905 to 1913 at the university.

Humans to Share the Earth

Across the Atlantic Ocean, Americans were relentlessly shooting, trapping, and poisoning bears, coyote, wolves, mountain lions, prairie dogs, and eagles. Wildlife in the early 1900s was to be "managed." Predators were seen as threats to man's interests and were to be exterminated.

By the 1930s ecological philosophers were enraged by the near extinction of wildlife, especially the bald eagle. The new concept of animals and humans co-existing in community was being advanced. Ecologists were studying the interdependence of human beings and creatures and nature. How could humans and wildlife share the earth?

Alfred North Whitehead (1861-1947) proposed that everything in the universe interacted and was dependent on everything else. Whitehead was an English mathematician and philosopher. His writings did much to narrow the gap between science and philosophy. He taught at London University before joining the faculty of Harvard University. Hence his works influenced both sides of the ocean. Whitehead reasoned that all forms of matter in the universe had a relationship to each other. Even the tiniest molecules are constantly interacting. It followed for Whitehead that every organism had special value because it contributes to the evolving reality of the universe. His writings led ecologists to a recognition that every being and physical element possessed important worth as it contributed to the components of what is called the global environment. Those who understood Whitehead's concepts were shocked at the futile killings of animals regarded as enemies or predators.

Schweitzer understood Whitehead's philosophy and the important worth of every organism. Later in his career he would expound on the reverence of life. Being a scientist and philosopher, he read the scientific works of Whitehead with a keen interest. Schweitzer also heard stories of mass animal killings in North America. He was disturbed by what he heard, although he had not yet fashioned his own ethics or personal response to the wildlife extinction.

A New Beginning

It is fascinating to see how Schweitzer, like Thoreau and Muir, broke sharply from his academic peers and the expectations of his society. He suddenly resigned his university appointments and turned his full attention to God's calling to serve the natives in what was then French Equatorial Africa. In 1913 he began serving at Lambarene. His first consulting room at this jungle hospital was a crude chicken coop.

In September 1915 Schweitzer found himself on a small steamer moving slowly up the Ogowe River. It was sunset, and the sounds of the churning engine disrupted the mood of the jungle wildlife. The boat had just passed through a herd of hippopotamuses. Schweitzer was on deck, deep in thought and almost oblivious to the surroundings, pondering a problem that had puzzled him for years: What was the most valid basis for all ethics? Suddenly, like a flash in his mind, the words appeared, *reverence for life*. This thought eventually was the cornerstone of his philosophy of living. He reasoned that every human being has a "will-to-live" which values, protects, and enhances life. He wrote extensively about how right conduct entails a reverence for the sacredness of life. He had a deep sense of awe and humility for the mystery and power of creation. This humbleness was often seen in his gentle manner with creatures big and small, human and non-human alike.

Love of Creation

Schweitzer was firm in his conviction that his reverence for life did not end with humanity. He looked beyond human relationships. This was another break in his thinking with peers. Conventional philosophers and theologians in Europe and North America concerned themselves with person to person relationships. Schweitzer began to write about love for *all* creation. Like Whitehead, he perceived how all elements of the universe were connected. *He believed that the ethical person respected the sacredness of all life: human and non-human species.*

Traditional philosophers challenged his values and ideals. Repeatedly he was asked how the ethical person can survive if there is a deep love for all creatures. How was this person to live? How could the person eat? Could such a person hunt to feed his family? Schweitzer wrestled with these questions and carefully reasoned things out. He answered these questions with the following thoughts: Human beings could, on occasion, kill other forms of life in order to live. But the taking of one life must be done only with a compassionate sense of responsibility for the life which is sacrificed. In all of his writings on animals, Schweitzer championed animal protection and the humane treatment of God's creatures.

Animal Welfare Award

Schweitzer's views on animals caught the attention of the world. By the 1950s, he was a man of many outstanding accomplishments, including building a large hospital and a medical station where thousands of Africans were being treated. He continued to publish books which had world appeal. Critics of his animal protection beliefs found it difficult to publicly attack the kindly old doctor who refused to step on ants. In 1951 the Animal Welfare Institute recognized his extraordinary effort in the humane treatment of animals. The Institute created the Schweitzer Medal, an official medal which honors individuals for their outstanding contribution to animal welfare. In accepting such esteem Schweitzer wrote to the Animal Welfare Institute:

> I am deeply moved that you would like to give my name to the medal you have created. I would never have believed that my philosophy, which incorporated in our ethics a compassionate attitude toward all creatures, would be noted and recognized in my lifetime. I knew this truth would impose itself one day on human thought, but it is the great and moving surprise of my life that I should be able to witness this progress of ethics.

Peacemaker

In the closing years of his life, Schweitzer proved to be an outspoken peacemaker. In 1952 he received the Nobel Peace Prize and used the $33,000 prize money to expand his hospital and set up a leper colony. In 1957 he went on record as opposing further atomic weapons tests because of the danger of radioactive fallout to humanity. He was well aware that his influence and reputation would give credibility to his peacemaking beliefs and values.

In reflecting on Albert Schweitzer's life and writings, I am always struck by how he carefully reasoned out ethical issues. He would ponder an ethical question for a long time before he would publicly voice his beliefs. He actively wrestled with issues on intellectual and emotional levels. He worked things through. Quite possibly this is why he felt so deeply about spiritual values, humanity, and animal welfare. His gentle spirit was no doubt guided by compassion, love, and values which had been carefully cultivated. Albert Schweitzer was able to live what he believed.

Aldo Leopold

"Man always kills the things he loves."

Our eco-values can change. As we examine our values and, in turn, live them, we can gain fresh insights into ourselves and the world around us. This may lead to cultivating new values and a deeper appreciation of life. Such was the curious journey of Aldo Leopold, an enthusiastic outdoorsman and naturalist. His early career in conservation expounded utilitarian values. Later he challenged these beliefs and risked personal change. He became known as the father of modern environmental ethics.

Leopold was born in comfortable circumstances in Burlington, Iowa, in 1887. He enjoyed hunting and had a strong interest in ornithology. Inclined toward an outdoor profession, he pursued it at Yale University, graduating from the School of Forestry with a master's degree in 1909.

America's Conservation Movement

There was a new, fresh air of conservationism sweeping the country at the time. President Theodore Roosevelt and his Chief Forester Gifford Pinchot had just succeeded in creating a concept to manage the earth's resources. In fact, the

Yale Forestry program owed its existence to the generosity of Pinchot. Understandably Leopold absorbed much of Pinchot's utilitarianism and the beliefs of other pioneer conservationists. Utilitarian philosophy believed that nature was to be used efficiently for the greatest good of the people. An added theme was proper wildlife management. This ethic was twisted and translated into a government policy of managing "good" animals (deer and cattle) and exterminating "bad" predators (chiefly mountain lions and wolves). It was believed that the greatest number of people could benefit from "good" animals.

An American Dream

I have found Leopold's background and early conservation career to be unusually interesting, especially when we see his later contributions to ecology. Here was a man who was a product of the American dream and societal values. He was reared in one of the greatest farming states in the United States, known as "the land where the tall corn grows." He was exposed to conventional midwestern values and as a youngster enjoyed fishing and hunting. The ideals of territorial expansionism were still being voiced as farmers plowed vast prairies and agriculture became the chief industry. Several Iowa cities were also noted for their cattle stockyards. Young Aldo's interest in the outdoors had several major influences. Yet at different periods of his life, he would seriously question—and challenge—many of his childhood beliefs and values about managing wildlife.

Life in the Wilderness

In 1909 Leopold left the comfortable and secure life of Iowa and was appointed a manager of national forests in New Mexico and Arizona. He faced a rugged, isolated lifestyle where he had to learn how to live with the creatures of the earth rather than enjoy creature comforts. He was eager to carry out his utilitarian policies. Actively engaged in hunting wolves and killing other predators, he envisioned national parks as vast areas for breeding healthy herds of game animals for the enjoyment of the human hunter.

Life in the remote forest in New Mexico gave Leopold his first opportunity to reflect on his values about the earth and wildlife. In many ways he was cut off from contact with people. He had time to read and think, although the remoteness also cut him off from diverse literature that was being published. He was familiar with the works of Thoreau and Muir. He enjoyed learning and reading and understanding ecology from different perspectives. He had an open mind to learning about wildlife from various writers and naturalists.

The Question

During the 1920s Leopold began to question the cherished belief of man's dominance over animals and the earth's resources. There was something unsettling about the prevailing standard that the earth fed humankind's physical needs and pleasures. He wondered if there wasn't a closer relationship between nature and humanity. He was also interested in the changing perception of the earth that considered the planet to be not a dead mass but rather dynamic and alive. This questioning left him with uneasy feelings about predator-extermination policies. He was left for a period of time in a great quandary about hunting and the utilitarian values which underlined the conservation ethics of the day.

Uneasy Feelings

The uneasy feelings that stirred Leopold moved him to seek out new knowledge about ecology and ethics. He was caught in a value conflict and he was astute enough to know that it would not be resolved unless he took appropriate action. Yet on several levels he was moving in uncharted waters. He realized full well that as an administrator in the

U.S. Forest Service he was obliged to carry out its orders and policies. Yet this created a value dilemma with other eco-values he was weighing. He recognized the importance of interdependency of organisms. How did this apply to oceans, forests, mountains, and wildlife?

He was at an impasse but he was also cut off from the ecology literature of the day. His isolated outpost did not have an outstanding university library that he was accustomed to use. Stop for a few moments and try to picture this ordeal in your mind. Let's face it. We are used to easy access to information and computer resources. It is, indeed, difficult to imagine Leopold's predicament.

New Ideas About Nature

In his search for help with these unsettled feelings and value discrepancies Leopold surprisingly discovered the writings of the Russian philosopher, Peter D. Ouspensky (1878-1947). Ouspensky held a conviction that nature was not simply divided between organic and inorganic. Nor was nature something mechanical that produced resources for man's creature comforts. The Russian philosopher wrote in *Tertium Organum* (1912 and translated into English 1920) that every tree, fish, plant, mountain, river, drip of water, and fire has a "mind" or spirit of its own. Everything in the universe had both a visible appearance and essence: life, feelings, or mind. A combination of objects made up communities and could be said to have life of their own. The whole (gestalt) was greater than the sum of the parts. Ouspensky believed that cells function together to make organs and organs make organisms possible. Leopold was impressed with these ideas and how they gave him a wider view of nature. Later, by 1933 as a professor of wildlife management at the University of Wisconsin, he echoed this theme. In his lectures he advised students to view the earth as a living system, akin to the human body, with interdependent organ systems.

The Earth as a Living Body

Leopold returned to the government argument recommending predator-extermination. Using Ouspensky's reasoning of the living earth, he proposed that if you eliminate one organ from the body, the body will eventually die. One of his favorite metaphors was to show what would happen to the "human body" (earth) if a surgeon eliminated the vital organs (ecosystems). Take away the heart or liver and a human being will die. Similarly, remove the heart from a wolf and it will die. Remove the wolf from the ecosystem and you change the interplay of the ecological community of which it is a part.

Land Ethic

Leopold developed an environmental philosophy that became known as the "land ethic." The care of the land ethic was a broad picture of a life community extending far beyond traditional dimensions. He perceived an ethical relationship to the community's different parts and to the whole. He had a broad or gestalt view of the earth. He feared that a strictly economic posture toward the earth created dire ecological problems. By 1930, he had broken away from the government view of exploiting the earth's resources. As he succeeded in his university career, he carefully blended science and ecological philosophy to advance his ideas about a living ecological community.

In 1933, Leopold published a paper, "The Conservation Ethic," in which he proposed the idea of ethical evolution. He observed the distinct parallels between human slavery and unconditional ownership of land. In the course of history, slaves were considered non-human. Abolition changed this. Accordingly, Leopold argued that the same ethical thinking was needed to liberate the land from human bondage and destruction. "The Conservation Ethic" joined with the ethical theory of Albert Schweitzer. The only difference was that Leopold used meticulous scientific facts to defend the rights of organisms and habitats. He provided a sound scientific foundation for the land ethic.

Environmental Education

During 1947 Leopold wrote *A Sand Country Almanac*, a collection of his thoughts and observations about nature and man's relationship to the physical world. The book was published after his death. In the book Leopold proposed that the role of human beings be changed from conqueror of the land-community to a citizen of it. *He wrote how humanity must respect the fellow-members (all races of peoples) and the ecological community (land, water, plants, wildlife, atmosphere, the stars).* To him, humans are members of an "ecology team." Yet as members, they have an ethical responsibility to justly use their technological power. In the final chapter of his book Leopold wrote that human civilization, with its advanced culture and tools, has abused nature because we have believed we are masters of the land. Yet when we begin to see nature as a complex, interdependent community to which we belong, we will then learn to share it with love and respect.

During his long career Leopold made significant contributions to the ecology movement, eco-values, and ethical theory. As an American thinker and naturalist, he affirmed Schweitzer's reverence-for-life principle. He argued passionately that *all* life needs to be respected. He believed that this fit his principle for respecting the web of life. He appreciated Chief Seattle's observation that humans do not weave the web of life, they are one strand in the whole web. Hence, individual organisms, humans included, were always subordinate in importance to the whole. This did not cheapen or lessen the dignity of humanity. Leopold simply dethroned mankind for the superior role it had presided over for centuries. He was realistic enough to know that it would take time for these value concepts to be absorbed by the American psyche.

Many historians have called Aldo Leopold the "Moses of the New Eco-Movement." They credit him with handing down the Tablets of the Ecological Law, but he did not live to enter the promised land. I believe this is a fitting testimony to a naturalist who wrestled with personal ecological value growth and thought. His legacy lives on in the popularity of his book, *A Sand Country Almanac*. What impresses me about Leopold is that he had a mind open to new ideas and values and beliefs. He was not afraid to question his own beliefs, no matter how he treasured them. As we examine our personal earth sensitive values, we can be reminded of the simple, yet significant, value of open-mindedness and the willingness to think in broader ways.

Rachel Carson

"Life is a miracle beyond our comprehension."

We all know that career and education plans are apt to change. The hallmark of a mature personality is flexibility and living up to one's God-given talents. Rachel Carson had childhood dreams of being a writer. She loved literature. Little did she know that her

burning ambition to write and her eco-values would catapult her onto the world stage of controversy to fight for the natural rights of insects and fragile ecosystems.

A Walk in the Woods

Carson was born in Springdale, Pennsylvania, on May 27, 1907. Quite simply, her love of the outdoors began in childhood. She enjoyed growing up in a rural setting where her family owned over fifty acres of woodlands. Her parents encouraged her to explore wildlife and to observe nature's moods and habits. As a youngster she had a special relationship with her mother, and the two developed a fond routine of taking walks in the woods to listen to birds. Quite frequently they rose before daybreak and trekked into the dark woods. Sitting quitely, they listened to life awakening and stirring around them. Rachel thereby developed a fine ear for identifying different bird sounds. This was both a skill and a love that would become part of a later crusade to passionately guard nature. As a youngster, this environmental activism was never part of her desires or even an awareness. She simply enjoyed the natural world, never realizing that it could be easily endangered by human interests.

College Years

Actually, Carson's life plans were wrapped up in literature and her avid interest in writing. By high school she had decided to major in English and attend Pennsylvania College for Women. To pursue this plan, she often spent her weekends in the library, studying and reading. This hard work earned her a scholarship to college. Once there, she participated in everything that had anything to do with writing and her major in English. She volunteered to work on the college newspaper and she also submitted many stories to the college literary magazine. She improved her writing skills and learned the value of persistence. Often she wrote and rewrote an article—and wrote it again—before it was accepted for literary publication. She learned the prudent lessons of reworking her creative ideas and also the virtue of patience. As we will see, these lessons came to fruition, and under fire, when she challenged the established practice of spraying the earth with insecticides. But this wouldn't happen until long after her college career took on another fascinating twist.

The Amazing World of Nature

Carson was required to take a science course before she graduated from college. To the budding writer, this was an utter waste of time! Biology was not in her vocabulary. Yet, if she had to take a science class, she wanted to enroll in one in which the instructor would keep her interest. At this juncture, she decided to take a biology course taught by

Miss Mary Skinker. To her amazement, the course opened her eyes and mind to the intricate world of botany and zoology.

Within a few classes, Carson became fascinated with biology and the enthusiasm of the professor. It was through her relationship with Miss Skinker that she made a critical life decision. She took a major risk and decided to abandon her career plans in literature and to pursue an advanced degree in science. She followed her instincts despite intense pressure from others to remain in English.

After her graduation from college, Carson earned the opportunity to spend a summer working on Cape Cod, Massachusetts. She worked at Woods Hole, home of the Marine Biological Laboratory. There she met the great scientists from all over America who gathered to study the complex life of the sea. This experience drew her toward the aquatic work that would eventually occupy her life. She felt at home by the sea, experiencing an inner peace. The summer internship also awakened in her a deep reverence for the earth's creatures.

New Challenge

By 1935, Carson had earned her master's degree in marine zoology. The Great Depression was still going on and she found it difficult to secure full-time employment. Then she heard that the U.S. Bureau of Fisheries was looking for a writer for a new radio program it was sponsoring. The program was called "Romance Under the Waters" and it involved broadcasting short stories about marine life. It was the first opportunity—and challenge—for Carson to combine her literary skills and knowledge of marine activity. She knew that the listening audience wanted more than a few dry facts about fish! The job excited her creative juices and she tackled the assignment with great enthusiasm.

Carson was the first woman scientist employed by the U.S. Bureau of Fisheries. She encountered the male "good ol' boy" system and initially wondered if she would be able to survive in the male-dominated bureaucracy. But she quickly discovered that she could blend her lucid prose with her affection for marine biology. After demonstrating success with the radio program, she was offered other writing assignments at the bureau. Her talent for making scientific facts come alive on the printed page was in demand.

The Writer

Carson was encouraged to submit articles on marine life to *The Atlantic Monthly* magazine. This popularized the public's interest in the sea, and the articles became the nucleus for her books *Under the Sea Wind* (1941) and *The Sea Around Us* (1951). The latter became an instant best seller and a Book-of-the-Month Club selection. *The Sea Around Us* revealed Carson's intimate knowledge of marine life and within six months was selling four thousand copies a day. With such popularity the Oxford Press decided to publish *Under the Sea Wind* again. The book that had been collecting dust since 1941 suddenly became a best seller in 1952. Thus two books by the same author were on a best seller list simultaneously, an unheard-of feat during that period. Carson thus knew that she could use her talent for writing and her love of nature to pursue other writing adventures.

Inner Reflection

In 1952 Carson was unsure of what would materialize. She wanted time to be alone and to think and plan. She resigned from her employment at the bureau. She could live on the royalties from the best sellers and simply take the time to daydream and write anything she wanted to write.

Her desire to go off and write was short-lived. Carson became a celebrity. Her name was famous, and as a lecturer and guest speaker she was honored at numerous autograph parties, receptions, luncheons, and dinners.

The Letter and Awareness

In 1958 Carson received a letter from a long-time friend, Olga Owens Huckins. The woman pleaded for the scientist's help. She explained how her community had been sprayed with DDT, a common practice to kill mosquitoes. The reportedly "harmless" shower bath had killed several lovely songbirds outright near the woman's birdbath. More died within a day. Olga wanted to know if Carson could contact some authority who would stop the dreadful killing.

Carson felt that her values had been assaulted. She was deeply moved by her friend's letter and request. As a scientist she knew first-hand what the woman had painfully described.

Poisoning the Earth

Carson's concern about insecticides actually dated back to the close of World War II. She understood that DDT was a potent poison and objected to such chemicals being called "pesticides," seeing a subtle human arrogance in the popular word. She believed that a creature was a "pest" only from the human viewpoint. In nature it had a legitimate role as part of what ecologists knew as the web of life. She preferred to call DDT and similar chemicals biocides or killers of life. And she knew that the "wonderful, magical" insecticides did not stop working at an expected point in the food chains. Creatures that consumed the poisoned insects became sick and died. Other species became unintended victims of the so-called harmless spraying. Ultimately the harmful chemicals infected the entire ecosystem. Insecticides were the deadliest thing man had ever spread across the earth. Carson could see a "silent spring" where no birds sang as a distinct possibility. And so, the scientist reasoned, ours was a sick human society, poisoned as an ironic side-effect of the relentless drive to conquer and subdue nature.

Silent Spring

At first Carson decided to write a brief book about chemical poisoning, and she started to collect the facts from different regions of the United States. The grim research data poured in. A cold chill crawled through her as she analyzed the reports. The most unthinkable consequences of DDT jolted her. Soon she was sending out hundreds of letters to scientists and ecologists all over the world. The evidence mounted against any rationale to justify indiscriminate spraying to control insects. The chemicals menaced the life and health of all species.

Rachel Carson was angry. She knew that her project would not be a brief book, and she decided to write a factual book that would shock America into awareness and action. It struck her that *Silent Spring* was the most appropriate book title. With earnest effort she collected irrefutable data. Her objective was to outlaw insecticides or at least greatly restrict their use. Like John Muir, she wanted to take the lead in the political arena. She knew she would lose her audience if she stepped too far ahead of public opinion. As a result she omitted any direct mention in *Silent Spring* of the rights of insects, fish, birds, and other victims of biocide. The only reference to natural rights is the author's suggestion that had our founding fathers been aware of deadly chemical insecticides they surely would have included freedom from poisoning in the Bill of Rights. When she described a poisoned ground squirrel writhing in agony, her point, like that of earlier humanitarians, was that such cruelty diminishes us as human beings. She avoided saying anything about the ethics of diminishing the squirrel.

Personal Tragedy

While Rachel Carson was writing the manuscript, her mother died. Their special relationship of mutual support and love abruptly ended. For weeks Carson was numb with sorrow. Consumed with grief, she could not concentrate on writing. Then she realized that she had to push herself to complete the book. Still, she felt tired. Something else was wrong. During the spring of 1960, she sought out doctors to find out why she was so tired. After several different medical consultations and operations she learned that she was suffering from cancer, but she decided to tell friends that she had arthritis, since she did not want people to pity her.

Carson forged ahead with her research and perspectives on man's relationship with nature. The final chapters were completed in 1962.

Conviction

The basis of Carson's ecological philosophy was her deep conviction that "life is a miracle beyond our comprehension, and we should reverence it even where we have to struggle against it." This Schweitzerian belief gives perspective to Carson's remark about humans needing "humbleness" and developing ecological values that stressed "sharing our earth with other creatures." *To Carson, any technological attempt to dominate and control nature could prove folly.* Insecticides with the rebounding consequences on human health was perfect evidence. In *Silent Spring*, Carson made it abundantly clear that human welfare, as well as the welfare of all living companions, was at stake.

A Nation Learns of Danger

Silent Spring shocked the nation. For the first time the public understood the serious health dangers of DDT and other insecticides. *Silent Spring* made headline news. It was like a shot that rang around the world. The insecticide business reacted with a volley of media reports defending their practice.

Carson refrained from verbalizing her real beliefs about the rights of nature. The closest she came to taking that step was on January 7, 1963, when she humbly accepted the

Schweitzer Medal from the Animal Welfare Institute. She was moribund at the time, her body depleted by cancer. This was a special moment for Carson. Schweitzer had been her inspiration. She had dedicated *Silent Spring* to him and to his conviction that people must restrain themselves or destroy the earth. At the ceremony, Carson observed how Schweitzer had reminded humanity that people become truly civilized when they value all life.

"Goodbye, My Friends"

Carson quietly retired to her home in Silver Spring. Her body was weakened and she was confined to a wheelchair. One night in April 1964, she instructed her nurse to wake her before dawn. The nurse obliged, and the following morning Carson asked to be wheeled out into the yard under the trees. There, alone, she listened and waited for the world to stir around her. Her trained ear strained to hear the first bird begin to chirp. She bid the birds farewell, and then died on April 14, 1964 at the age of fifty-six.

Legend has it that President Abraham Lincoln once remarked to Harriet Beecher Stowe, "So you are the little lady who started this big war." The author of *Uncle Tom's Cabin* argued that blacks were not commodities to be exploited but fellow members of the human community. The idea was like a lit match and it sparked a revolt that blew the United States apart at the seams.

Rachel Carson was the little lady who lit the fuse to another war—the battle against the careless use of deadly chemicals. *Silent Spring* argued that all life species, even insects, were not commodities but deserved ethical consideration. Her book was a catalyst for a new environmental ethic sweeping America at the time.

Carson's achievements and gifts to humanity are many: she was the first female scientist in the U.S. Bureau of Fisheries, the disciplined author who opened America's interest in and love of the sea, and the heroine who used her final energies to fight for the rights of insects and fragile ecosystems. Certainly we can admire her for her feisty and sincere dedication to the reverence for all life.

Carson provides us with another example. She shows what it means to be flexible in life, to be willing to follow one's values, to take a risk and change. Prior to the Great Depression, when people clung to any security, this was a courageous leap of faith.

The lives of St. Francis, Thoreau, Muir, Schweitzer, Leopold and Carson allow us to see ecological values in action. Although these individuals lived in different periods of history, they shared a common desire to know and live their personal values. What made this possible? I feel that they all had certain gifts and strong traits that allowed them to journey into the unchartered waters of life. These include:

Open-Mindedness—an ability to go beyond conventional thinking. Each recognized that there are different ideas and sources of knowledge about the earth. They were open to explore new beliefs about human values and nature.

Willingness—a readiness to act without reluctance. Each promptly responded to the needs of the earth and, also, of fellow human beings. They were willing to sacrifice material things in order to pursue a deeper meaning to life.

Awe and Wonder—a recognition that life is both a miracle and mystery. Each person believed that God's creation is a precious gift and joy.

Spirituality—a belief in the power of the divine creator and a desire to have an intimate relationship with the creator. While each person had different religious affiliations, all were open to meditation, thanksgiving, and prayer. They realized that their stewardship was to fulfill the will of the Father on earth. Their spiritual values were hope-filled.

Humility—the acknowledgment that humanity does not control or rule over nature but is a part of the bigger picture. All of them showed the virtue of humility in their daily lives.

Daring—an ability to take a leap in faith and to change one's ideals, values, and lifestyle. All of them were willing to lose personal status, even in the face of criticisms, and to follow their eco-values. They were risk-takers.

Take time to reflect on these gifts. What can you incorporate into your own behavior, attitudes, and values? How can these qualities help guide your journey into new challenges and opportunities with ecology?

Part Four
Resources

"Whatever befalls the earth befalls the sons of the earth.
Man did not weave the web of life,
he is merely a strand in it.
Whatever he does to the web, he does to himself."
—Chief Seattle

Eco-Resources

When people come together to discuss a problem, new ideas and new solutions are generated. When people exchange ideas they network. Networking is a way to solve problems. Networking occurs between groups of people, and also among organizations. Networking provides opportunities for working with larger environmental organizations and sharing updated information on environmental action. Networking is a thread which helps to heal the ruptures in the web of life.

You and your family and friends can use a variety of environmental resources and networking opportunities. You may choose to join an environmental group. You can obtain the organization's newsletters and publications. You may check out local resources: church, library, nature centers, and educational institutions for environmental pro-

grams. Your city might sponsor an annual clean-up campaign or beautification program. There are endless ways to get involved.

The following pages provide a listing of environmental organizations whose interests lie in saving and preserving the earth. Each offers a variety of activities that encourage members to become actively involved, network, and exercise activism.

There are many companies that supply cruelty-free cosmetics and personal care products. Their products have not been tested on animals. Check the list of cruelty-free shopping resources in this section.

Resources are tools we need to get a job done. Environmental resources increase our skills so that we can help make this a better world.

Student Environmental Organizations ————————————

North American Students of Cooperation (NASCO)
P.O. Box 7715, Ann Arbor, MI 48107
Purpose: Sponsors educational programs for schools and ecology clubs.

Student Conservation Association (SCA)
1800 N. Kent St., Suite 1120, Arlington, VA 22209
Purpose: Dedicated to environmental education and volunteer opportunities in conservation projects. Volunteers serve in national parks and forests, wildlife refuges and other conservation areas nationwide.

Student Environmental Action Coalition (SEAC)
National Office: P.O. Box 1168, Chapel Hill, NC 27514-1168
Purpose: Dedicated to educational and activism opportunities for young adults. Publishes *Threshold*, SEAC's national student environmental magazine. Regional offices provide resources and information for a unified student environmental movement.

National Environmental Groups ————————————

American Forestry Association
P.O. Box 2000, Washington, DC 20013
Purpose: Dedicated to improving the health and value of trees and forests and sponsors community regreening programs. Currently working on Global Releaf, and international campaign to encourage tree planting to help curb the effects of global warming.

Animal Welfare Institute
P.O. Box 3650, Washington, DC 20007
Purpose: To eliminate suffering inflicted on animals and to educate the public on the humane treatment of wildlife. Publishes *The Endangered Species Handbook* which contains projects for classrooms and science fairs.

The Cousteau Society, Inc.
930 W. 21st Street, Norfolk, VA 23517
Purpose: Dedicated to the protection and improvement of the quality of life; produces television films and research on ocean life and coastal wildlife.

Defenders of Wildlife
1244 Nineteenth Street, NW, Washington, DC 20036
Purpose: Dedicated to protecting and preserving the diversity of wildlife and plant biospheres. Sponsors an "Action Alert" program for grassroots activism and letter writing campaigns to help save endangered species.

Greenpeace USA, Inc.
1436 U. Street, NW, Washington, DC 20009
Purpose: Works to protect the environment from nuclear and toxic pollution, and to stop the threat of nuclear war. The award-winning *Greenpeace* magazine is published on a bimonthly basis.

International Network For Religion and Animals
P.O. Box 1335, North Wales, PA 19454-0335
Purpose: Enhances the role all religions play in improving our treatment of animals and nature. Provides educational programs for church and community groups.

National Audubon Society
950 Third Avenue, New York, NY 10022
Purpose: Advocates the wise use of land, water, wildlife, and other natural ecosystems. Sponsors the study of bird life and migration patterns. Currently working on wetlands protection and activism to preserve the Ancient Forests and Arctic Nation Wildlife Refuge. Provides educational programs for high school and college students.

National Wildlife Federation
1400 Sixteenth Street, NW, Washington, DC 20036-2266
Purpose: Undertakes a comprehensive conservation education program, distributes periodicals, sponsors Earth Day activities, and helps to settle environmental disputes. Currently working on energy policies, environmental quality,

and wetlands protection. Provides educational programs for high school and college students.

The Nature Conservancy

1815 North Lynn Street, Arlington, VA 22209

Purpose: Works to develop a network of international programs to preserve nature sanctuaries. Manages a system of over 1,100 nature sanctuaries and diverse biosystems. Encourages volunteer participation. Call (800) 628-6860 for further information.

Rainforest Action Network

301 Broadway, Ste. A, San Francisco, CA 94133

Purpose: An activist organization dedicated to saving the world's rainforests. Currently working on protecting rainforests in Hawaii, Amazonia, and Southeast Asia. Volunteer positions are available.

Sierra Club

730 Polk Street, San Francisco, CA 94109

Purpose: Promotes the responsible use of wild places and seeks to protect the quality of the natural and human environment. Sponsors Earth Day activities and other educational programs for youths and adults. Currently working on wilderness/desert/national park protection. Extensive volunteer opportunities and grassroot activism available throughout the country.

Community Groups ─────────────────────────

America The Beautiful Fund

219 Shoreham Building, Washington, DC 20005

Purpose: Supports new, local action projects aimed to improve the quality of the environment and community living.

Keep America Beautiful, Inc.

9 West Broad Street, Stamford, CT 06902

Purpose: Dedicated to improving waste handling practices in American communities. Encourages home and community recycling and public education programs on beautification.

Regeneration
33 East Minor St., Emmaus, PA 18098
Purpose: Dedicated to improving the quality of community life; publishes a bimonthly newsletter with numerous suggested family and community projects. Provides information on alternative methods to pesticide-free gardening and lawn care.

Renew America
1001 Connecticut Ave., NW, Ste. 719, Washington, DC 20036
Purpose: Supports renewable energy projects, home and community recycling, and water conservation. Currently promoting a "Searching for Success" program which honors those working to solve environmental problems.

Social Action Groups

Food For The Hungry
7729 East Greenway Rd., Scottsdale, AZ 85260
Purpose: Christian organization founded to combat hunger and to provide local churches with fund-raising ideas and speakers for hunger-related topics.

The Giraffe Project
P.O. Box 759, Langley, WA 98260
Purpose: A national organization dedicated to inspiring people to stick their necks out for social action and the common good. Sponsors grassroots projects for high schools and colleges.

The Learning Alliance
494 Broadway, New York, NY 10012
Purpose: Provides current information on a wide range of community and

social issues, including peace, race relationships, the environment, homelessness, and community health and economies.

Conservation Groups ——————————————————————

American Rivers
801 Pennsylvania Ave., SE, Ste. 400, Washington, DC 20003
Purpose: Dedicated to protecting and restoring the nation's rivers and ecosystems. The organization has effectively preserved over 10,000 river miles for clean water and scenic beauty. Currently working on protecting wild and scenic water systems.

The Izaak Walton League of America
1401 Wilson Boulevard, Level B, Arlington, VA 22209
Purpose: Dedicated to the wholesome use of our natural resources and clean water projects. Uses grassroots political activism to influence governmental policy-making. Sponsors the "Save Our Stream" program which helps to monitor stream pollution and fight sources of environmental damage.

Trout Unlimited
501 Church St., NE, Vienna, VA 22180
Purpose: Dedicated to the protection of clean water and enhancement of trout and salmon fishery resources. State and local chapters available. Publishes literature aimed at promoting responsible fishing and outdoor activities.

The Wilderness Society
900 Seventeenth Street, Washington, DC 20006
Purpose: Dedicated to protecting wildlands and wildlife and safeguarding our federal public lands and national forests. Currently working on protecting the Arctic wildlife refuge and developing a national forest policy.

World Society for the Protection of Animals
29 Perkins Street, P.O. Box 190, Boston, MA 02130

Purpose: Dedicated to international animal protection and wildlife conservation. The only international animal protection organization with consultative status with the United Nations.

Xerces Society
10 SW Ash St., Portland, OR 97204
Purpose: Working locally and globally to prevent human-caused extinction of rare invertebrate populations and their habitats. Promotes annual butterfly count. Currently working to protect the Pacific Northwest old-growth forests.

Political Action Groups

Environmental Defense Fund, Inc.
257 Park Avenue South, New York, NY 10010
Purpose: Pursues responsible reform of public policy in the fields of energy and resource conservation, toxic chemicals, air quality and land use.

National Alliance for Animal Legislation
P.O. Box 75116, Washington, DC 20013-5116
Purpose: Dedicated to protecting animal rights and sponsoring legislation for humane treatment of animals.

National Resources Defense Council
40 W. 20th St., New York, NY 10011
Purpose: To protect America's natural resources and improve the quality of the human environment. Combines legal action, scientific research, and citizen education in a highly effective environmental protection program.

For Recreation and Fun ———————————————

American Hiking Society
1015 Thirty-First Street, NW, Washington, DC 20007
Purpose: Formed to educate the public on the responsible use of foot trails and to protect the interests of hikers.

National Campers and Hikers Association, Inc.
7172 Transit Road, Buffalo, NY 14221
Purpose: Dedicated to the education of the public concerning the need for conservation of natural resources.

National Parks and Conservation Association
1015 Thirty-First Street, NW, Washington, DC 20007
Purpose: Promotes a healthy national park system and encourages family trips to national parks.

Rails-To-Trails Conservancy
1400 Sixteenth Street, NW, Suite 300, Washington, DC 20036
Purpose: Works with local recreation and conservation groups to preserve our nationally built rail system for recreational uses (hiking, bike trails, etc.)

Educational Resources

As we have already seen, environmental education can be obtained in many different ways. The same is true for gaining an understanding of ecological values. There are several educational resources that offer a variety of workshops, educational experiences and that also publish literature for young adults and families. They blend learning about ecology with human values.

Alliance for Environmental Education
10751 Ambassador Drive, Ste. 201, Manassas, VA 22110, (703) 335-1025
Purpose: To serve as an advocate for a quality environment through a network of educational programs throughout the country.

Center for Environmental Information (CEI)
46 Prince Street, Rochester, NY 14607, (716) 271-3550
Purpose: Established to provide comprehensive information on environmental issues. CEI offers education programs, publications, and information services.

Institute for Earth Education (IEE)
P.O. Box 288, Warrenville, IL 60555, (509) 395-2299
Purpose: Disseminates educational programs and literature and hosts international and regional conferences.

National Audubon Society Expedition Institute
P.O. Box 170, Readfield, ME 04355, (207) 685-3111
Purpose: Graduate, undergraduate, and high school education programs which offer year-long and semester expeditions providing an alternative to traditional education that emphasizes ecological education.

Cruelty-Free Shopping

Many communities avoid animal testing or animal ingredients in their products. Write and ask for information about their products.

Beauty Without Cruelty, USA
175 West 12th St., #166, New York, NY 10011-8275

The Body Shop
Hanover Technical Center, 45 Horsehill Road, Cedar Knolls, NJ 07927-2003

The Compassionate Consumer
P.O. Box 27, Jericho, NY 11753

Humane Alternative Products
8 Hutchins St., Concord, NH 03301

My Brother's Keeper
211 South 5th Street, Richmond, IN 47374

Environmental Films

Voices of the Land, 20 minutes
A film by Christopher McLeod
Distributor: Bullfrog Films, (800) 543-FROG. This film examines how the destruction of sacred land also means the destruction of the human spirit.

Power To Survive, 29 minutes
A film produced by Shauna Garr
Distributor: New Day Films, (212) 645-8210. Four minority teenagers voice their concern about pollution, crime, drugs, and poverty.

Spaceship Earth: Our Global Environment, 25 minutes
A film by Kirk Bergstrom
Distributor: World Link, (213) 273-2636. A film designed to inspire and motivate teenagers about environmental problems.

To Protect Mother Earth (Broken Treaty II), 60 minutes
A film directed by Joel L. Freedman and narrated by actor Robert Redford
Distributor: Cinnamon Productions, (212) 431-4899. This award-winning film is a story of the Shoshone struggle to save their lands from oil drilling and nuclear tests.

Where Have All The Dolphins Gone? 48 minutes
A film by Sam LaBudda and narrated by actor George C. Scott
Distributor: The Video Project (415) 655-9050. A film that documents the failure of U.S. government laws to protect marine mammals.

For more information about environmental films, contact: *Environmental Film Resource Center,* 324 N. Tejon St., Colorado Springs, CO 80903, (800) 7ENVFILM.

RESOURCES   **173**

Environmental Music

American Gramophone Records
9130 Morman Bridge Rd., Omaha, NE 68152, (402) 457-4341
Series: Nature Sounds
Description: Recording of music played during benefit concert with Chip Davis
and a variety of classical music selections.

Celestial Harmonies
P.O. Box 30122, Tucson, AZ 85751, (602) 326-4400
Series: *Sacred Ceremonies: Ritual Music of Tibetan Buddhism*
Description: Music explores the vibrant sounds of the monks' ancient musical
meditations.

Dan Gibson Production
U.S. Distributor: Northwood Press, (800) 336-5666
Series: Solitude Series
Description: Recorded series of nature soundtracks, featuring a large variety of
North American environments.

Four Winds
P.O. Box 1887, Boulder, CO 80306, (800) 456-5444
Series: Kevin Locke Series
Description: Award-winning music based on ancient flute songs.

The Nature Company
2001 Western Ave., Seattle, WA 98121, (206) 443-1608
Series: Environmental Sound Series
Description: Pure environmental sounds combined with synthesized sounds.

Rykodisc
Pickering Wharf, Bldg. C., Salem, MA 01970, (508) 744-7678
Series: Environmental Sounds
Description: Music captures natural sounds of the rainforests.

Silver Wave Records
P.O. Box 7943, Boulder, CO 80306, (303) 443-5617
Series: Nature Sounds
Description: Recorded in Australia, combines music with nature sounds.

Sound of America Records
P.O. Box 8606, Albuquerque, NM 87198, (505) 268-6110
Series: Environmental and Native American
Description: Music defines native American issues.

Talking Taco Records
P.O. Box 40576, San Antonio, TX 78229-1576
Series: Flute and Nature Sounds
Description: Native American flute music inspired by traditional sounds.

Wild Sanctuary Communications
124 Ninth Avenue, San Francisco, CA 94118, (800) 473-WILD
Series: Habitat Series
Description: Music combines contemporary music with nature and animal sounds.

Publications

Carson, Rachel. *Silent Spring.* Boston: Houghton Mifflin, 1962.

50 Simple Things You Can Do To Save the Earth. Earth Works Group. Berkeley: Earth Works Press, 1989.

Fraser, Laura, et al. *The Animal Rights Handbook.* Los Angeles: Living Planet Press, 1990.

Hollender, Jeffrey. *How To Make the World a Better Place.* New York: Quill, 1990.

Leopold, Aldo. *A Sand Country Almanac.* New York: Ballantine Books, 1966.

Seymour, John and Girardet, Herbert. *Blueprint for a Green Planet.* New York: Prentice-Hall, 1987.

The Student Environmental Action Guide. The Student Environmental Action Coalition. Berkeley: Earth Works Press, 1991.

One thing that always amazes me is the number of ways to learn about ecology in my community. Just when I think I've identified what is available, I will talk with someone and learn about a new film, wildlife art festival or public presentation. At one time in my life I wasn't aware of any of these events. They always existed. I just didn't pay much attention to what was going on. This changed after our family got on the mailing list of a local nature center. Now we look forward to the bimonthly newsletter listing field outings, film presentations, nature walks, and speakers. You may also be surprised to find that there are many learning opportunities at your local museum, community college, humane society, church, and nature center. One final suggestion: Don't forget to talk with people who belong to Audubon groups. They often have an uncanny mental directory of resources and a calendar of events!

Ten Eco-Ideas

1

Did you know that many of our states are experiencing severe water shortages? Conserve water by not allowing it to run needlessly when you shower, wash the car, or work in the kitchen.

2

Did you know that emissions from power plants contribute to acid rain and the greenhouse effect? Help conserve energy by turning off the lights when you leave a room.

3

Did you know that there are no boundaries to environmental action? You can get involved with ecology activities at school, at church, and in the community. Check the phone book for ecology groups in your area. Talk to biology teachers for more information.

4

Did you know that cars are the biggest source of greenhouse gases? Bicycles do not pollute the environment. Promote bike riding at school and safety education for bicyclists.

5

Did you know that schools can be called "paper mills"? Look at the amount of notebook paper, old reports, exams, and computer paper that gets dumped. Suggest that your school start a paper recycling program.

6

Did you know that Americans throw away more than 870,000 pounds of food each day? How much of your school's food waste comes from student trays? Live by the motto, "Take only what you can eat."

7

Did you know that school bookstores can carry earth-friendly products? Encourage your school bookstore to carry environmental books, recycled paper products, environmental calendars, and T-shirts.

8

Did you know that what you eat and how it's grown have an impact on the earth? Many foods are grown with pesticides. Add organic foods to your diet. Help reduce pesticide use.

9

Did you know that billions of beverage containers are overflowing in our landfills? Recycle aluminum cans. If possible, buy beverages in refillable bottles.

10

Did you know that yard waste and food leftovers are filling up landfill space? Waste can be composted. Start a composting program at home and school.

SCRIPTURE-SPEAK

"Be doers of the word, and not hearers only" (Jas 1:22).

Bibliography

Bodo, Murray. *Francis, The Journey and the Dream.* Cincinnati: St. Anthony Messenger Press, 1972.

Carson, Rachel. *Silent Spring.* Boston: Houghton Mifflin, 1962.

Carter, Jimmy. *An Outdoor Journal.* New York: Bantam Books, 1988.

Cornell, Joseph. *Sharing the Joy of Nature.* Nevada City: Dawn Publications, 1989.

Leopold, Aldo. *A Sand Country Almanac.* New York: Ballantine Books, 1966.

Lewis, Hunter. *A Question of Values.* San Francisco: Harper and Row, 1990.

Linzey, Andrew and Regan, Tom. *Animals and Christianity.* New York: Crossroad, 1990.

Mills, Stephanie. *Whatever Happened to Ecology?* San Francisco: Sierra Club Books, 1989.

Muir, John. *Wilderness Essays.* Salt Lake City: Peregrine Smith Books, 1980.

O'Connell, Brian. *Finding Values That Work.* New York: Walker and Company, 1978.

Schweitzer, Albert. *Reverence for Life.* New York: Harper and Row, 1969.

Thoreau, Henry David. *The Selected Works of Thoreau.* Boston: Houghton Mifflin, 1975.

Van Matie, Steve and Weler, Bill. *The Earth Speaks.* Published by the Institute For Earth Education, 1983.

Weiner, John. *The Next One Hundred Years.* New York: Bantam Books, 1990.